It's Not
What You Say...
It's What You Do

It's Not
What You Say...
It's What You Do

HOW FOLLOWING THROUGH AT EVERY LEVEL CAN MAKE OR BREAK YOUR COMPANY

Laurence Haughton

CURRENCY
DOUBLEDAY

New York   London   Toronto   Sydney   Auckland

"A teacher affects eternity: he can never tell where his influence stops."
Henry Adams

This book is dedicated to all my teachers—from both the
formal classroom and the school of hard knocks—and
especially my consulting partner and mentor Jason Jennings.
Your lessons have affected me and I am forever grateful.

A CURRENCY BOOK
PUBLISHED BY DOUBLEDAY
a division of Random House, Inc.

CURRENCY is a trademark of Random House, Inc., and
DOUBLEDAY is a registered trademark of Random House, Inc.

Book design by Chris Welch

Library of Congress Cataloging-in-Publication Data
Haughton, Laurence.
It's not what you say— it's what you do : how following through at every
level can make or break your company / Laurence Haughton.
p. cm.
1. Management. 2. Management—Case studies. 3. Success in business.
I. Title.
HD31.H659 2005
658.4'01—dc22
2004056115

ISBN 0-385-51041-1
All Rights Reserved
PRINTED IN THE UNITED STATES OF AMERICA
First US Edition: January 2005

SPECIAL SALES
Currency Books are available at special discounts for bulk purchases for sales
promotions or premiums. Special editions, including personalized covers,
excerpts of existing books, and corporate imprints, can be created in large
quantities for special needs. For more information, write to Special Markets,
Currency Books, specialmarkets@randomhouse.com.
1 3 5 7 9 10 8 6 4 2

Contents

Introduction

■

HOW FOLLOWING THROUGH AT EVERY LEVEL CAN MAKE OR BREAK YOUR COMPANY

A team of researchers put 160 big companies under a micro-scope. Their objective was to find the answer to a pair of burning questions:

Why do some companies *consistently* outperform their competitors?

Which strategies and tactics, among the hundreds recommended by management gurus and experts, actually *make the difference*?

Calling themselves The Evergreen Project, the researchers began by sorting all 160 organizations into 40 industry-specific groups—each with similar scale, scope, finances, and future prospects. Next, each company's ten-year track record was analyzed and all the firms were divided into one of four categories:

- *Winners,* who consistently outperformed their competitors
- *Losers,* who fell short time after time
- *Climbers,* who started off poorly but found a way to improve dramatically
- *Tumblers,* who began with a definite advantage and went south

The experts then cross-referenced the strategic plans at each of the companies with two hundred-plus high-powered tactics. All the brightest ideas were on the list—from "Customer Relationship Management" to "Six Sigma," from "360-degree Feedback" to "Enterprise Resource Planning."

By reviewing both the performance records over ten years and the strategic choices among all the popular initiatives, the research teams were able to separate cause and effect. In other words, The Evergreen Project identified which of these business strategies made a substantial impact on a firm's competitive advantage and which didn't.

The final conclusion surprised everyone involved. "It matters little whether you centralize or decentralize . . . if you implement ERP software or a CRM system," wrote the leaders in their final analysis,* "it matters very much though that whatever you choose to implement you execute it flawlessly."

Conventional wisdom is wrong. Becoming a winner, a loser, a climber, or a tumbler in any industry is *not* the result of finding (or failing to find) the perfect strategy for your organization. What makes or breaks a company's performance is its grasp over management's most basic mission—to make sure everyone at every level *follows through*.

That's not as simple as most executives expect it to be.

As fast as most managers learn their first lessons from the school of hard knocks, they discover there's a gaping hole in their company's day-to-day operations.

> Half of all the decisions a company makes in order to solve some problem or take advantage of some opportunity will fall through the cracks in less than two years . . . not because of uncontrollable factors like a recession, unexpected cost hikes or any other outside factors but simply from a lack of follow through.†

*N. Nohria, W. Joyce, and B. Roberson, "What Really Works," *Harvard Business Review*, July 2003.
†See this research from Ohio State's Fisher College of Business in the section "More Accurate Assessments."

And a 50 percent failure rate is for the *average* company. As one telecom executive said when he heard that stunning statistic, "After spending twenty-five years working in the high-tech sector, in my experience, that number is too low."

This book tells the stories of a unique group of managers who've cracked the code on following through. Working in all kinds of organizations—public and private, large and small, new economy and old, even highly bureaucratic government agencies and entrepreneurial start-ups—these leaders have discovered step-by-step solutions for taking whoever falls below them on the organizational chart, be it a team, department, division, region, or entire company, to a new level of thoroughness and reliability under the toughest competitive conditions. They learned to overcome the obstacles that cause so many of management's best intentions to slip through the cracks, and then they shared their insights in great detail so anyone can follow in their footsteps.

Their stories and the lessons learned are organized into four "building blocks," the components crucial to following through:

1. Having *a clear direction* so everyone understands where they're headed in no uncertain terms.
2. Matching *the right people* to every goal.
3. Getting off to a great start with plenty of *buy-in.*
4. Making sure everyone maintains their momentum by increasing *individual initiative.*

Building Block I
Clear Direction

No executive intends to start off an initiative or business with vague, assumed, or conflicting expectations. They all start out intending to convey their expectations with absolute clarity. But under the pressure of too little time and too much to do, under pressure from unspoken, assumed directives from bosses, customers, and other departments, many managers decide that because people are nodding their heads they have all they need in terms of a clear direction. And when later they see that their people have made little or no progress, they don't retrace their steps. Instead, they falsely assume "that strategy wasn't right for our company."

This building block provides the tools for turning vague, general, or conflicting expectations into clear, specific, and coordinated targets. It shows how to quickly connect the dots and anticipate what people need without them telling you. You'll also learn a three-step system that will help your people consistently make the best decisions.

Building Block II
The Right People

Experts who specialize in turnarounds agree. When asked, "If you were about to take charge of a business, where would you begin?" they replied, "With the people." "You can have the best product or service, a great bottom line," said one, "but without the right people from top to bottom, it is impossible to follow through."

This building block will show how to match your people to your expectations. You'll find fresh ideas to guarantee better follow-through in fast-changing situations. One example? Hire attitudes over experience. Another is that great teams make sure everybody is on the *same page*.

And there's even a section upending the conventional wisdom about who should manage the follow-through and exactly how you can make sure you are choosing the right leader for every project.

Building Block III
Buy-in

Conventional wisdom says that when your reasons for changing directions are well-communicated and your plan is solid, the majority of people will buy in automatically. But conventional wisdom doesn't match up to reality. More often than not, no matter how well a leader communicates his or her rationale, or how intelligently he plans, or how much participation she facilitates, the typical response of people in business is *not to buy in*.

Whether you're executing a major change strategy or implementing day-to-day directives for improving your product lineup; your plant and equipment; your pricing, personnel, or management policies, customer service, etc.—include tactics for getting enough buy-in to overcome the law of inertia.

Here I'll show you how to outmaneuver the opponents to change that inhabit every organization and come up with a plan for getting everyone to just let go of old ideas and worn-out ways. There are also lessons for turning your people into a HOT team and your managers into HOT team leaders.

Building Block IV
Individual Initiative

Character is the ability to maintain momentum long after the mood has passed.

I've used that quote to inspire myself and others. My intent has been to link the loss of momentum to a lack of character so that people see not following through as a personal flaw. But I now have learned that interpretation missed a more valuable insight.

Leaders must endeavor to do everything in their power to keep people *in the mood* to follow through. That means developing the management tactics that guarantee more individual initiative.

This section presents three simple strategies for unleashing and focusing the character in every person on your team:

1. Creating a *reason* to rise above tough conditions and taking the initiative necessary to make sure what's expected gets done.
2. Recognizing the vital role shows of respect play in generating more individual initiative.

3. Realizing that deciding who's responsible isn't a panacea and that there's a fine line between enough and too much accountability.

Over the last decade, business has tried every quick fix and crafty financial maneuver to get a leg up on the unrelenting competition. None of it has had sufficient staying power and a lot has landed our businesses (and more than a few executives) in trouble. Now it's time to forgo all the exotic answers and get back to basics. What makes or breaks your company is your ability to get everyone at every level following through. This book shows you clearly what to do.

Laurence Haughton
Fall 2004
lrh@laurencehaughton.com

Building Block I

■

CLEAR DIRECTION

D oes every employee *understand* where your business is going?

Are the steps necessary to reach each goal *plain to see?*

Is there a *good line of sight* between your company's mission and what your people do?

Finally, does your team *support* the direction of the business?

Forty-eight percent of the 12,000-plus top executives, middle managers, and front-line employees surveyed for WorkUSA 2002—Watson Wyatt's annual research report on employee attitudes—could not honestly answer *yes* when asked those questions.

If Wyatt's research report accurately reflects the American workplace, almost half of all employees feel they are working without a sense of clear direction. No wonder it's so tough to make sure what's expected gets done. It's the simplest of all business calculations—if people don't understand precisely where they are headed, it's only sheer luck that will get them to where they need to be.

This failure to create a clear sense of direction is not from a lack of trying. "We work longer and harder now than ever before on making our messages [about strategy and direction] connect," a vice president from a major financial services firm said. "Truth be told, however, we still probably miss half of the time . . . or at least it feels that way to many out and away from command central."

Why? Providing a clear direction these days is difficult.

• *People are vague.*

Customers, coworkers, investors, and even many top corporate executives—the very people who insist that your business unit follows through and meets all their expectations—are often unclear, contradictory, and inconsistent.

• *Time is short.*

Over three-quarters of all managers are making more decisions per day than they were in 1997. But only 15 percent of those managers have been given any extra "think" time.

• *Processes are flawed.*

Two-thirds of all day-to-day directional issues—about new products, staffing, policy changes, price increases, etc.—are determined using decision processes prone to fail.

In the next three chapters, you'll learn what to do to overcome these obstacles and consistently give your associates a clear direction.

First, in "Clear Expectations," I'll offer a prescription for how to turn vague, general, or conflicting expectations into clear, specific, and coordinated targets—even if you're the manager stuck in the middle between headquarters, staff, and customers.

Next, in "Read Between the Lines," I'll show you how to quickly connect the dots between what people say and what they really want, without them telling you in an overt or explicit manner.

Finally, in "More Accurate Assessments," we'll hammer out a system for thinking things through more thoroughly (even under tight deadlines) and fine-tuning your directions with tactics prone to *succeed.*

1 CLEAR EXPECTATIONS

One day, executives at a multinational company presented their annual operating plans (AOPs) and budgets to the top brass. The CEO then followed up with a critique of their plans and a list of his expectations for the upcoming year. Here are some excerpts:*

- "We need an ambitious plan for productivity that overachieves the target."
- "Our quality problems are disturbing. Continue to work to improve quality."
- "Good work on reducing past-due shipments. However, past-dues are still among the highest in the company, so opportunity remains."
- "Cost reduction is a big opportunity for you. One point of cost will take you from an uncomfortable position to a comfortable one."
- "[For next year] build a plan that allows you to react to different scenarios, given the high level of economic uncertainty."

The memo went on like that for seventeen bulleted points. A few

*Adapted from *Execution,* by L. Bossidy and R. Charan, Crown Business, 2002.

focused on products: "We need to drive better results out of product line Z"; a few on people: "Work with executive A to crisp up your plans"; and the remaining ones on company initiatives: "Put more focus on Six Sigma." The CEO concluded with a thank-you: "Overall, you had a great AOP presentation last week." He suggested the executives meet with him in ten days to "discuss the specifics of how we will achieve [each of the] targets."

The author of that memo is Larry Bossidy, the former CEO of Allied-Signal and one of the best of the best CEOs. Bossidy knows a lot about getting things done, a skill he's demonstrated many times at Allied-Signal and through his best-selling book *Execution*. Undoubtedly, Bossidy wrote this memo to make sure each manager clearly understood what he expected so their follow-through would be flawless.

But does his memo really spell out *just what's expected?*

Linda Lockwood of Charles Schwab and Company, Inc., reviewed the excerpts and asked herself that critical question. Lockwood is a vice president and chief of staff at Schwab. In her fourteen years in financial services, Lockwood has also built a great reputation for getting things done—and in the last few years she's worked especially hard on the skills and disciplines for starting every initiative with crystal-clear expectations.

"No," Lockwood said. "I would say most managers would look at this and quickly dismiss it as the same old corporate gobbledygook."
Specifically:

- *Our quality problems are disturbing. Continue to work to improve quality.* "Where's the bar?" Lockwood asks, wondering how any manager could tell when they had achieved his objective. "And what's the connection between quality problems and the preceding directive, 'We need an ambitious plan for productivity that overachieves the target'? Could productivity and these 'disturbing' quality problems be connected?" she added. "I wonder how thoughtfully each of these goals was integrated?"
- *Good work on past-due shipments. However . . . opportunity remains.* "This is a completely mixed message," according to

Lockwood. "An employee reading this would feel momentarily good, then bad and then confused—never knowing exactly what was expected."

- *One point of cost will take you from an uncomfortable position to a comfortable one.* "This one is hilarious! A comfortable point for me is on a sailboat leading the pack," she said with a smile. "Seriously, *uncomfortable* is subjective. The reader would have no idea how to measure the specific outcome."

Call them goals, targets, objectives, key results areas, it doesn't matter; management's expectations must be like a lighthouse, a bright and focused beacon that guides the team's follow-through, signaling which direction to head in. If those expectations are vague, confusing, or incompatible ("corporate gobbledygook" in Lockwood's words), the next level of managers and their associates are more likely to make the wrong turns at critical junctions or simply, in bewilderment, stop following through.

In this chapter, you'll learn the essential disciplines for starting with clear expectations. Moreover, I'll show you how you can take a boss's vague, general, or conflicting directives and make them clear and focused.

THE PRESCRIPTION

Lockwood has seen many vague, general, and conflicting directives over the years in her company. That's what motivated her and others at Schwab to develop a prescription for making sure that expectations are clear and capable of guiding follow-through.

First, Lockwood said, "Each goal needs a crisp, measurable definition of success with a timetable and point person or department responsible for the follow-through." It's not good enough to give people fuzzy or universal pronouncements like "we need to improve customer satisfaction." Satisfaction must be deconstructed into all the little pieces that add up to a satisfied customer, and then each element must be made measurable.

Second, "The manager needs to look over what is expected to

weed out conflicts between one objective and the next. For example, if the team sets 'ambitious plans for productivity,' " Lockwood asked, "can they also be nimble reacting to different scenarios?"

The best way to discover if these two goals conflict is for the manager and the team to brainstorm all the ways they might improve productivity and what it takes to be nimble. Then the manager and some coworkers should imagine where the two goals might clash.

For example, one answer for greater productivity might be to cut the cost of production by using the least experienced (and therefore lowest-paid) person to do a job. But being nimble may require that someone with higher skills (and a higher salary)—such as the ability to improvise or to anticipate different scenarios—should do the work. Maximum productivity could conflict with maximum agility.

"If two expectations clash," Lockwood has learned, "then priorities *must* be clarified and set."

Finally, Lockwood concluded, "Every expectation needs check points embedded in the goal to make sure things are getting done, and if not, to give the team a chance to adjust before time expires."

Lockwood's common sense approach to starting with clear expectations isn't news. For years, experts in goal setting have suggested managers use the acronym SMART as a checklist for issuing clearer goals and targets. SMART stands for *s*pecific, *m*easurable, *a*ccountable, *r*ealistic, and *t*ime-bound. Managers who check every expectation to make sure it's SMART could avoid giving their people any *corporate gobbledygook*.

But equally important as making expectations SMART, Lockwood believes, is managers who ensure that everyone on the team *gets* the message.

"There needs to be a sophisticated, cascading communications plan for each manager," Lockwood said. Her group at Schwab uses these four guidelines to make sure their expectations are clearly communicated:

- **Divide big ideas into palatable bites.** "Goals must cascade [flow] throughout the organization," Lockwood said. They can't be communicated the same way to everyone. Clear expectations require a manager to break complex goals into palatable bites, appropriate to the mind-set of each team member.

"Everyone is not a gold-medal performer," she continued. "Companies need the silver- and bronze-level players to follow through as well. Even nickel players are required, so leaders must make sure what they expect is explained in a manner that can be understood by every level of associate."

- **Get feedback.** "Executives can easily lose sight of the various levels of employee thinking/knowledge/perspective," Lockwood observed. "They need effective mechanisms for staying in close touch with their employees."

To clearly communicate expectations at a big company like Schwab, the top brass relies on a tightly integrated team of corporate communications, public relations, and human resources experts. Those communications specialists in turn rely on carefully constructed and constantly updated employee surveys to get feedback from everyone at the front lines.

In smaller companies and those without in-house surveys, a leader needs to find someone who can give them honest feedback on their communications. It can be as simple as asking a teenage member of your family, or a friend's son or daughter. One executive recalled how he got help from a sixteen-year-old: "She read what I wrote and said, 'Sometimes I think you say certain things just to show how smart you are.'" The executive realized how this kind of frank and candid critique could help him communicate more effectively. He asked the young woman to read his entire memo and mark every sentence that struck her that way. Her honest feedback made a huge contribution to the executive's clarity.

- **Be a hands-on executive.** Staying engaged is essential to ensuring that expectations are clearly communicated. "So often they [executives] delegate too much and lose the pulse of the business," Lockwood said. "I still delegate, but I balance that with my need to keep connected.

"At first blush, people might think, 'Oh, this is a harder person to work for than one who's more hands-off.' Actually, in my personal experience," Lockwood explained, "it is more rewarding and, in the end, easier to work for someone who is engaged and demanding accountability because you know where you stand and you are better armed to succeed."

- **It's not what you say but what you do.** Executives must communicate what they expect through what they do, demonstrating their own command of the details and a commitment to consistent follow-through to their teams, according to Lockwood. "This means more work, but that's why executives get the big bucks," she said. "There's nothing like follow-up by an executive, if it's the right follow-up on the right objective. It's incredible what respect and desire to work harder are generated when an executive demonstrates these behaviors to their employees."

Setting smart expectations and disciplining your communications plan so each goal is clearly understood will guarantee you are giving your people clear expectations. But curing your own lack of clarity isn't enough in the vast majority of organizations. Eighty-eight percent of all employees work in enterprises with more than one layer of management. These multiple layers make setting and communicating clear expectations more complicated, especially for the managerial leader stuck in the middle.

STUCK IN THE MIDDLE

"How can I give clear direction to my team when my organization's senior leadership is fuzzy [regarding what they expect] and the big picture doesn't get communicated?" Pat asked, frustrated. Ever since a big international conglomerate purchased his business unit, Pat has been stuck between his desire to meet customer, coworker, and corporate expectations and the lack of clear and consistent direction from the top layers at headquarters.

For example:

- "We want you to respond faster to local needs. Prepare your yearly budget and as long as you are meeting your targets, you are free to run things as you see best." Yet even though his teams hit their budgets, the next level of management above Pat continued to intervene in his decisions and micromanage the team's efforts. "Do they want us to wait for instructions and their blessing before we do anything, or do they want us to be fast and autonomous?" Pat wondered.

- "Tell your people to talk honestly and directly. We want open communications." But when one of Pat's managers tried to be honest and open during a company meeting, Pat said, "those same senior managers branded the guy a negative person." That branding got back to the manager during a performance review (when he asked why he was turned down for a promotion) and sent a mixed message to everyone in the unit.

What's a manager like Pat supposed to do when he or she is stuck in the middle between the need for clear expectations to drive the follow-through and vague, confusing, or inconsistent direction from the top? I would argue they have three choices:

- **Let things from headquarters fall through the cracks.** One manager in Pat's situation said he just ignores all the confusing directives he gets from headquarters until somebody calls to yell at him about something. "That's the only way I can figure out what they really want out of all the stuff they ask me for. Honestly, 75 percent of the time I never hear another word."

- **Tell the boss straight out, "Your directives are ambiguous."** "I've gotten frustrated and done that," Linda Lockwood admitted. "My manager at the time didn't miss a beat. 'Hey, it's your job to figure that out,' he told me," and Lockwood was left where she started.

Or you can:

- **Take charge**—and get the clear direction you need by negotiating your boss's expectations.

NEGOTIATING EXPECTATIONS

"Over years of trial and error, I've learned I can't throw up my hands, I can't use blunt objects to beat clarity out of my manager, and I can't let it roll downhill to affect my people and their follow-through," Lockwood explained. "So I've learned how to go back again, again, and again to find out what success looks like through their [the boss's] eyes."

What Lockwood does is called negotiating expectations. Not "negotiate" in the *you can negotiate anything, start high and don't give away the store* meaning of the word. It's negotiating as in "to successfully travel along or over,"* to cross the distance between vague, confusing, or unspoken expectations and get to clear, actionable, synchronized targets. Negotiating expectations is an expedition, where everyone reaches clarity together.

For example, Lockwood said, "I'll go in and say, 'I think this plan delivers on your directive. Here's my criteria and how I plan to measure each deliverable. Does that look good to you?' It's an iterative process. I stay engaged until I get the clear and measurable answers. Then I have the clarity I need without resorting to blunt objects."

There are two skills you need for negotiating expectations with superiors:

1. Get them engaged, and then
2. Listen

1. GET ENGAGED

"There are two reasons I believe a manager avoids producing clear expectations, besides the fact they may not know how," Lockwood explained. "Either they are:

a. overwhelmed with responsibilities or
b. they don't want to commit because their manager wasn't clear with *them* and they are worried about being held accountable."

In both cases, your boss is likely to say that he or she doesn't have the time to discuss the directives further. If they do this, *don't back down.* Instead, get them engaged in your process of negotiating expectations.

Nobody is better at getting busy executives engaged than Jason Jennings. Jennings is an author and keynote speaker. In the last two years, he has climbed to the top strata of lecturers hired to address

Merriam-Webster Online Dictionary

business conventions and conferences. Jennings's success has been driven by his determination to exceed the expectations of those who hire him. To do this, he has learned how to engage them.

"Every meeting planner, conference director, and CEO has a different idea of what they want from their keynote speaker," Jennings said. "And they never make it clear." His years of experience enable him to infer some of what they want, he said. But unless he has a *complete* picture of what they expect beforehand, he doesn't have the edge he needs.

"I like to have a big standing ovation, and I want the CEO and the organizers to lead that applause," Jennings revealed. To get that, Jennings always sets up a conference call in advance with the president or CEO. "In that call I get them to completely clarify their expectations," Jennings said.

A lot of the time all Jennings has to do to set up this call is to ask. CEOs and organizers readily agree, because Jennings follows a couple of cardinal rules for getting them engaged. First, he gives the CEO a clear idea of *what's in it for them*. Second, he makes sure the process creates *no more work* for the executive.

"That's all it takes 80 percent of the time," Jennings explained. "In the other 20 percent, I get a meeting planner or PA who still says, 'Oh, the CEO is too busy.' I know then I have to convince both the planner and the CEO that it's worth their time to talk to me. My best tactic is to tell them this story:

> I was one of three keynote speakers at a huge $6 million conference for Yellow Corporation. There were three keynoters to kick off the conference—me, Rudy Giuliani, and Jim Collins.
>
> Yellow had just invested hundreds of millions of dollars transforming the company from an old-line trucking operation to a modern logistics and solutions business. The purpose of the day was to cement new attitudes among the workforce and top clients at the conference, attitudes that reflected Yellow's new strategic positioning.
>
> To introduce the day, the planners had brought in the president of a national trade group. He was going to do fifteen

minutes just before my keynote. It quickly became clear that this guy from the trade association hadn't learned anything at all about Yellow's transformation. He had just prepared his standard shtick.

The trade group president approaches the mike at center stage and looks out to the assembled two thousand key employees and top clients. "Good morning!" he roars. "There's no place I'd rather be right now than hanging around with a bunch of truckers."

At that moment, I'm standing backstage next to Yellow's chairman, Bill Zollars, and I see the color start to drain from his face.

The speaker continues his warm-up: "And they can call me anything, including the CEO of the trade association, but I'm an old huckster just like you and I love to peddle stuff."

Zollars is now beside himself. He leans over and whispers to me, "Jennings, you're up first—can you fix this? This guy is starting our $6 million event in the absolute wrong direction." Happily, I was able to undo the damage, but I've never forgotten the look on the Zollars's face. The first speaker could have ruined the conference!

I've seen too many events where a speaker not only didn't deliver all the organizer wanted but their comments were contrary to the long-term interests of the company. The easy way to make sure that never happens is to have a short conversation. I've got four simple questions that I've learned will eliminate any miscues and let me exceed your expectations. When is it best to talk—now or later this week?

Jennings tells this story as a last resort to make the risks of *not* talking to him before the conference real and substantial.

As a result, he always gets the time he needs from even the busiest CEOs and directors.

You need your own story to get senior executives who resist your direct request to clarify their expectations. Your story will help you "sell" your boss. Think about a time an initiative went wrong because the goals were misunderstood or because everybody didn't start on the same page. Put the story together as Jennings did, showing them some risks they can relate to, and do it all in ninety seconds or less. You'll get that senior executive engaged.

2. LISTEN

Remember, there are a couple of reasons most executives don't give clear direction:

- When an executive is unclear, perhaps it's because they are overwhelmed.
- An executive may be trying to avoid accountability because their boss wasn't clear with them.

Each is a potentially embarrassing admission, one any manager would discuss freely only with a trusted associate. That makes building trust an imperative for negotiating expectations.

Most trust builds slowly, taking months and years of interactions. However, research shows that when people are in a situation where they need assistance they will quickly extend a form of trust, called "calculated trust," to someone who exhibits the right behavior.

Calculated trust is decided with a simple checklist. "Does the other party," the potential trustee asks:

a. share my values,

b. speak my language, and

c. listen to me?

If they get three yeses on that simple list, most people will extend calculated trust. That's why it's so important that you work very hard on your listening skills. Only through effective listening is it possible to demonstrate that you share values and "speak the same language."

DOS AND DON'TS

When getting ready to ask your boss about his expectations, use the following guidelines:

Prepare. Nobody is that good on their feet. Ask questions at the right time. Maintain a feel for their comfort and the level of openness. *Do* your homework. Get the facts and piece together everything you can find out from other sources before you sit down to talk. Ask your questions flatly without any signals that their answer might be sensitive or none of your business. It is always a surprise how much someone will tell you if you just ask. *Do* be persistent if they avoid giving you the whole story. Remember, figuring out just what they expect is in everyone's interest, especially theirs.

Don't ask anything antagonistic. Erase the words "blame" and "fault" from your mind. *Don't* stop listening to think about the next question. Be prepared in advance, and make a note if something comes up you want to ask about. *Don't* cross-examine; this is not a courtroom. You are there to show them you are both on the same side. *Don't* show how smart you are by answering your own questions. They are the only ones who know the bottom line—get *them* to tell *you*. *Don't* be afraid to take notes if necessary. You don't want to miss anything. *Don't* censor yourself. Have a face-saving recovery comment for questions the other party deems none of your business.

LISTENING IS HARD WORK

Most people are poor listeners. Within minutes of any oral presentation, half of what was said has gone in one ear and out the other. After forty-eight hours, three out of every four facts have been totally forgotten. Why? Most people mistakenly think that being a good listener is all about keeping quiet and waiting until the other side stops moving their lips. But people who depend on their listening skills for a living will tell you listening is a lot more than *not* talking. Listening is a practiced discipline requiring training, enormous concentration, and energy.

The average person talks at a rate of 135 words a minute. But the average person comprehends at over four times that rate. So while one is listening, their mind races ahead—sandwiching other thoughts in between the ones being expressed by the speaker. Those extra thoughts can distract the listener just enough to miss a few of the key signals (an implication, a look of anxiety, or something subtle that changes the meaning of the word just spoken). Distracted listeners get easily confused, asking the wrong questions at the wrong time, and the dialogue becomes a lot less productive.

Test your ability to listen on an associate or subordinate before you meet with your boss. Interview an associate about their goals/expectations for their career and record your conversation. When you play the tape back, you'll be surprised at how much more you get out of the conversation the second time through. (And you'll be embarrassed that your questioning wasn't better.)

Professional listeners use several techniques to get more out of every conversation:

- They make a point of collecting and remembering questions and comments that succeed in getting people talking.
- They get in sync with the speaker, changing the pace and tone of the conversation to reflect the style of the person they're talking to.
- They pay close attention to expressions, tone, and gestures.
- They signal that they are actively listening to keep the other side involved by:

  Following up with relevant questions

  Summarizing constantly what's been said during the conversation

  Challenging and probing deeper

- Last, they emphasize shared values and work to use shared language. (In other words, they signal, "I'm like you, you're like me, therefore you can trust me.")

CLEAR EXPECTATIONS ARE CRITICAL

According to Dr. Elliot Jaques, a renowned author of fifteen books on organizational theory, giving people clear expectations is more than a good idea, *it is the reason that managers exist.*

In *Requisite Organization,* Dr. Jaques explains that the manager's role in large, multilayered, competitive businesses is to make things clear. "We define a manager as a person who is held accountable for the outputs of others and for sustaining a team capable of producing those outputs. [That] manager must be able to add value to the work of immediate subordinates."

Value is added, says Dr. Jaques, when the manager creates an "effective context" for employees.

It's simple. If a manager doesn't (or can't) create an effective context for those below them on the organizational chart, they aren't adding any value. If they aren't adding any value, that layer of management is unnecessary.

What's the surest way for a manager to create an effective context and add that value?

By making all expectations crystal clear. How can you do this? Here's a recap:

1. Set *SMART* goals. Every goal needs a crisp definition of success. Each should be specific, measurable, accountable, realistic, and time-bound. Find the time to clarify your own expectations before you ask others to follow through.

2. Communicate more *effectively*. Expectations aren't clear until everyone knows the steps they're required to take and how that connects with the team mission. Managers must divide big goals into palatable bites, right for every layer below them on the organizational chart.

3. When you're stuck in the middle . . . *negotiate*. What do you do when the expectations you are given are fuzzy and ambiguous? You understand why a boss isn't always clear and do something about it; get them engaged and listen.

2 READ BETWEEN THE LINES

So here's the apparent contradiction in most companies:

One   Clear expectations are a critical first step in creating a clear direction.

Two   Customers, coworkers, company investors, and even many top corporate executives—the very people who insist that a business unit delivers flawlessly on their expectations—are often vague, contradictory, and inconsistent.

The key to resolving this contradiction is to create clear expectations. This involves asking lots of questions, methodically listening to the answers, and then going back again and again until you understand.

But this process can take a lot of time—time to ask the right questions and time to reflect on the answers. And time, as everyone knows, is short.

There is a skill good managers and executives use to ensure that they understand the expectations of customers, coworkers, and senior executives quickly. It's called "reading between the lines."

In this chapter, I'm going to demystify this intuitive recognition of what people expect and lay out the steps you can take to improve your ability in this area.

READING BETWEEN THE LINES

Some managers have developed a real aptitude for reading between the lines. John Borthwick is one of them. Borthwick is a senior VP at Time Warner's Office of Alliances and Technology Strategy.

In May of 2000, Borthwick got a call from his boss, the vice chairman of AOL, Ted Leonsis. Leonsis had been stuck in his car for two and a half hours on an L.A. freeway. "Why can't I listen to my e-mail messages on my phone?" Leonsis demanded to know.

Borthwick knew his boss wasn't suggesting his phone was defective, but that Leonsis wanted Borthwick to investigate the possibility of a new service allowing AOL members to hear that familiar "You've got mail" even when they were far away from their computer. Reading between the lines, Borthwick knew he was being charged with a major new initiative.

Within three weeks of that call from Leonsis, Borthwick had a prototype version of AOL by Phone (a service whereby AOL members can hear their e-mail messages—the text message is converted into an audio file). He then took the prototype to senior executives and got a green light (and millions of investment dollars) for making the service a reality. Borthwick took the new service from prototype to market in just four months.

That incredible pace wasn't due solely to Borthwick's (and his team's) brilliance as innovators. What helped speed their follow-through was Borthwick's ability to read between the lines to discern the wants and needs of AOL members, technology partners, and senior executives at (then) AOL Time Warner, without having it all spelled out explicitly.

For example, Borthwick used three intuitions to make sure that the top bosses would buy into his proposals:

1. **Be ready to explain yourself five or six different ways.** Borthwick often has to explain his idea to an executive who can only see things from one perspective—like how a new product or service will appeal to Wall Street or help cut costs.

   Borthwick has learned to put himself in the shoes of executives from several different departments (legal, marketing, finance, investor relations, etc.), so he can convey his ideas in words and examples they readily understand and show how the product benefits their areas of interest.

2. **Align your innovation with the current corporate priorities.** Every company has to please many masters. Management is worried about the opinions of financial analysts, the media, customers, senior executives, and their peers. And each department or division is affected by ever-changing factors, requiring follow-through that can turn on a dime.

   When Borthwick began working on AOL by Phone, it was intended to be a new pay service. But then the priorities changed as Bob Pittman (one of AOL's top people then jockeying for a top spot in the postmerger AOL Time Warner) was looking to make the rollout of AOL 6.0 a huge success. Borthwick, reading between the lines, adjusted the features of AOL by Phone so that it could be bundled into AOL 6.0 at a minimal cost, helping Pittman achieve his goal.

3. **Always show a tangible display or prototype.** Senior executives will never *say* they are impatient with conceptual discussions and uncomfortable when asked to use their imaginations. But as he watched managers at AOL review proposals, Borthwick sensed their discomfort during such discussions. He realized that he had a much better chance of getting busy top executives to sign off if he gave them something they could touch. So he started prototyping every proposal before submitting an idea for executive approval.

Borthwick didn't come up with these guidelines through questions and answers, or by being told what to do in a memo. He read between the lines during his interactions with senior executives and intuitively understood this was the way to get their approvals.

Borthwick used this same intuitive ability to help him understand exactly what an AOL customer would want in an e-mail-by-telephone interface.

- He knew without being told that AOL's members expected easy navigation. Those intuitions led Borthwick and his team to research the way engineers used sound to help blind people "see" their way around the Windows operating system and how fighter pilots use 360-degree sound to update their mental picture of the airspace during an enemy attack. Each of those scientific advances made a contribution to the prototype for AOL by Phone.

- Borthwick also used his intuitions to assess the three target companies that could give AOL the software engine necessary to bring AOL by Phone to market. His top prospect was the highly regarded leader in voice technology. This company had the backing of several big venture-capital firms and an energetic group of young executives. Their product was fully developed and ready for market. Acquiring them would cost a couple of hundred million, but Borthwick had the money.

However, Borthwick's intuitions told him to look past the specific technology to the attitudes of the tech company's key executives. Experience had taught Borthwick that "If it works . . . it's obsolete," meaning every invention must be made better constantly or it will become outdated. He put himself in the shoes of a twenty-five year old in charge of a start-up technology company who's been told their invention was worth $200 to $300 million (this was before the Internet bubble burst). Borthwick didn't believe any kid pumped up by fawning venture capitalists would have the humility necessary to take an invention through the rigors of continuous improvement.

So he rejected his most obvious choice and put together a deal with a smaller (and significantly less expensive) Canadian company, called Quack, run by executives in their middle thirties who, he felt, would likely have a more mature attitude about the need to keep working hard on their innovations. Borthwick's intuitions were right on the mark. Top executives at AOL called his acquisition of Quack an "undiscovered gem."

While Borthwick's intuitions are finely tuned and reliable, they aren't a magical ability or a rare aptitude. Everyone has the same capacity to read between the lines.

IT'S CALLED THE EMPATHY EFFECT

Think back to the last time you met new people at a parents meeting at your child's school or at a cocktail party after an industry conference. With your social antennae extended, you probably noticed a lot of things that ordinarily you would have overlooked—another person's body language, choice of words, tone of voice, and any inconsistencies. Even the smallest detail told you volumes. One research project determined that the average person is able to make ten significant determinations about another person, from trustworthiness to educational level, without the other person even opening their mouth.

Psychoanalyst Heinz Kohut called the source of these intuitions "empathy." Kohut defined empathy as "the capacity to think and feel oneself into the inner life of another person."* Empathy provides an individual with reliable intuitions about the feelings, thoughts, and experiences of another *without* having those feelings, thoughts, or experiences communicated in an objective or explicit manner.

Empathy is not sympathy. Empathy allows you to maintain objectivity. You are able to empathize with people you don't necessarily like, drawing conclusions reached without your own emotional baggage. Kohut thought that this objectivity made empathy a critical skill for a psychotherapist.

Empathy is just as important for managers who need reliable intuitions about what others expect so that they can create a clear direction for their team's follow-through.

How Does Analysis Cure? by Heinz Kohut, University of Chicago Press, 1984.

LEARNING TO EMPATHIZE

Richard Coraine has made it his business to learn how to generate a high degree of empathy in himself and in his 650 employees. Coraine is the director of operations and managing partner of the Union Square Hospitality Group in Manhattan.

Union Square's restaurants are not the trendiest, the most convenient, or the fanciest. Yet, year after year, several are voted among the twenty *best* restaurants in New York by a panel of 25,000 fiercely independent critics. In 2003, Union Square captured both the number 1 and 2 positions as the "most popular" in the Zagat guide to New York restaurants.

The Union Square Hospitality Group distinguishes itself from its 2,000-plus competitors by practicing "enlightened hospitality"—a real-time, intuitive recognition of a customer's expectations, followed by an effort to *exceed* those expectations. Here is how Coraine illustrates Union Square's practice of "enlightened hospitality":

> A man booked a table with us for what he said was a very important business meeting and our people immediately started to read between the lines. They imagined how anxious he was likely to be to impress his prospective clients, so they arranged to hold a nice table away from the busiest parts of the lunch crowd without being asked.
>
> When this customer arrived, our reservations person noticed another opportunity [for more enlightened hospitality]. The grip was broken on his valise and our guest held it under his arm so his clients wouldn't notice. So while the two ate lunch, we sent the bag around the block and had the strap reattached.
>
> As he came to the front to check out, our host handed him his bag by the grip so he could see it was good as new. No one said a word.

Gourmet magazine writer Bruce Feiler tied the practice of "enlightened hospitality" back to the idea of empathy in his article

"The Therapist at the Table": "To work here [at the Union Square Café, one of the organization's six venues] is to discover your inner therapist . . . to spend an enormous amount of time thinking about other people—not just what they need but what they feel." Manager Lauren Grazer adds, "Often the nicest things we do for guests are the things they don't even know about [or know they want]."

"Put yourself in someone's shoes," is what Coraine tells employees, "and you'll understand instinctively what you have to do to make them feel special." Coraine's partner and the company's founder, Danny Meyer, sets the bar of enlightened hospitality high. "We are in business to create raves for the people with whom we have transactions," he tells employees. "If they say '[it was] fine,' that was *not* a rave."

To develop the empathy required for enlightened hospitality, Coraine created a recipe for becoming more empathetic.

Coraine's Recipe

Do you remember the conclusion of the film *The Wizard of Oz*? As the Wizard is preparing for his trip back to Kansas, he looks out at the assembled crowd and makes an announcement:

> And I hereby decree that until what time—if any—that I return, the Scarecrow, by virtue of his highly superior brains, shall rule in my stead . . . assisted by the Tin Man, by virtue of his magnificent heart . . . and the Lion—by virtue of his courage! Obey them as you would me!

According to Coraine, that final proclamation contains the three ingredients needed to make anyone more empathetic: smarts, heart, and courage. Coraine then goes on to tell another story:

> I had just flown from New York to Atlanta and got to the hotel right after midnight. I hadn't eaten on the plane and thought I just needed a light snack before I went to sleep.
>
> I called down for room service and asked for a bowl of chicken soup and crackers.

Something, I don't know what, made the young woman on the other end ask me a question completely disconnected from my request.

"Are you feeling okay?" she inquired. "That's an order I get when somebody isn't feeling well."

"No, no, I'm fine," I said, clearing my throat. "Thanks for asking. I just got off a plane from New York and I have an early-morning business meeting. I'm hungry and I'm tired, but I'm fine."

She could have followed the hotel's procedures manual, saying, "Bowl of chicken soup, crackers, room 1125. That will be up in twenty-five minutes. Is there anything else?"

But she used her head, thinking that a guest calling for chicken soup and crackers and sounding like he's half asleep might not be feeling well.

Then she used her heart, which said, "If I wasn't feeling well, I sure would want someone to ask about me and show they care. I'll just see if there is something more I can do to make him feel better."

Then she had the courage to act on what her head and heart had told her.

"I'm glad you're not ill," she said. "But still I'm going to put a note on this order to get everything to you quickly so you can have your soup and get to sleep fast."

I'll bet that young lady makes about eight or nine dollars an hour. Yet she did more to reinforce that hotel's brand with me than a million-dollar TV commercial. I totally experienced her heart. I totally experienced her intelligence. I totally experienced her courage to act. And I raved to everyone in my company.

Coraine wrapped up the story as he does for every employee. "You have to use your *head* and be curious. You have to use your caring *heart*. And you got to have *courage* to go out of your way for people you've never met," he explained. "That's what you need for empathy."

USE YOUR HEAD

When Guy Archbold took over as CEO of BluePoint Energy, Inc., it was a start-up on the verge of shutting down. But in just two years he turned it around.

Internally, the organization is much improved—the staff has been reenergized, the patents are now approved, and the prototypes surpassed all technical expectations. Externally, the future is bright—many new investors have opted in, strategic alliances have been inked with Fortune 50 partners, and customers have made significant commitments. While a lot of work remains, the change has been dramatic.

Tom Manz, one of the original investors, said he was amazed at what Archbold was able to accomplish. The reason? Archbold had never before pulled a venture back from the brink. He's never even worked at a technology company. He's a former Wall Street money manager and executive.

"Guy learned the science, defined the market, got conversant in the lingo, and lined up a string of alliances with quality partners like So Cal Gas," Manz said. But what really amazed him was Archbold's ability to pull all the people together crucial to BluePoint Energy's future.

"Archbold is a magician," Manz continued. "He connected with high-level investors, hesitant utility executives, and engineers as skeptical as you could imagine. He brought them all to the point where they could see past the problems to the big possibilities and got them committed to follow through. I've never seen anything like it. He [Archbold] turned around some very difficult people."

How was Guy Archbold, a former Wall Street money manager, able to win over so many diverse groups? "Suits from Wall Street have never been widely successful interfacing with anyone but other Wall Street suits," Manz observed. "Guy could get down with the mechanics at a utility and up to the highest-level financial or managerial strategists and everywhere in between. He made them all believe."

"All I had was half a solution and had to scramble for the other half," Archbold admits. "I needed some magic." The magic came when he used his head for empathy.

What do I mean by that? Let me explain with another story.

Like all the original investors, Archbold had bought into Blue-Point Energy's exciting innovation—plug-and-play electrical generators that would do for the old-line utilities business what desktop PCs did for the computer business. It would transfer power (literally) into the hands of the people and create a revolution of reliable, low-cost, nearly pollution-free electricity.

"California had just gone through the worst electricity crisis in a lifetime," Archbold explained. "Pundits had predicted brownouts and massive rate increases as far as the eye could see. I saw a chance to get involved with some new technology destined to remake a multibillion-dollar industry—and capture a huge chunk of the profits." When the investors signed on, they were told, "The technology is ready for patent application, the projected manufacturing costs make each unit a bargain [the generator would pay for itself in twenty-four months], and commercial interest was sky-high."

But the investors weren't given the whole picture. There were big holes in the technology blueprint to which the company didn't own the solutions. "We were blinded by the possibilities," Archbold admitted. "We relied on the word of the chief engineer/systems designer and found he didn't have all the pieces. I was severely disappointed."

The investors needed to make a decision. "Our choice is to let this thing go *kablooey* before it sucks in any more cash, or decide this is where we want to make a stand and do what it takes to follow through on the original vision," Manz said, characterizing the situation.

The group decided to follow through. Archbold took over as CEO with one immediate goal: stitching together enough of a success story to attract additional investors. This was the first big test of Archbold's ability to use empathy.

"I'd say it was a 'show me' marketplace when I first went out to see investors and potential partners," Archbold explained. "Venture capitalists had long since said, 'Forget good ideas. Show me your sales . . . preferably profitable sales.' Executives from the major utilities and influential consulting engineering firms I needed for my alliances were of the same mind. *Show me* was the universal response from the market. My problem was I had nothing to show them."

Archbold read between the lines and recognized that what the venture people wanted was a high-return investment that was virtually risk-free. If BluePoint's technology was patent protected and the company had enough customer interest to show even a small profit, the risk to investors would be very low.

Archbold's ears told him that a "no-risk deal" was what investors wanted. But his head for empathy told him many would settle for something less. Any savvy investor understands that high rewards are always accompanied by higher risks. Archbold's intuition told him that if he could show investors that BluePoint Energy was less risky than other start-ups, that would be enough to earn their trust and get them onboard.

He decided to test that intuition by creating a word-of-mouth campaign. His goal was to prove that BluePoint Energy was on the verge of being a big success.

Here's how he did it:

Anytime Archbold talked to a potential purchaser who said, "Guy, we want to buy one hundred of these things. It's in our plan to try this out in the next twelve months," Archbold would send the prospective buyer a follow-up e-mail. The e-mail would say something like "Dear Larry—Great to talk to you today. As per your request, I will call with our test results the moment they are in. I appreciate the confidence you have in us. I am very happy to hear your plans include one hundred of our units in the next twelve months—blah, blah, blah."

Typically, he would get an e-mail reply that read something like "Yes, Guy, it was good to hear your progress. As we discussed, I want our consulting engineers to review your test results the moment they are ready."

Then Archbold would forward that message to his potential investors and partners.

"I did the same with positive feedback from municipalities, consulting engineers, big names like So Cal Gas; I also forwarded the reports that projected a bright future for distributed generation [as the industry was now called]," Archbold explained. "I'd forward messages about my progress to my stakeholders time and time and time again. I must have done that a thousand times."

These e-mails weren't the patents or the profits investors and partners had said they expected before they committed, but they were the next-best things—tangible evidence of BluePoint's potential.

"This drip, drip, drip of good news was incredibly effective," Archbold said. "People stayed committed even as we experienced some more bumps along the road."

At one point, BluePoint's investors were told to expect sales of the first ten units by May. The rollout hit an unexpected snag and by August the company had failed to deliver even one.

"It would have been easy for some of the [investor] group to pull out," Archbold said. "It was, as I said, a *show me* environment. But the deal closed with everyone in, because my e-mails *showed them* enough evidence of the coming success to feel confident about our momentum.

"Everyone got the macro view [the big picture]—positive industry trends, hundreds of commitments, and a long line of what I called virtual sales. The next-best thing to a risk-free venture was a constantly progressing, reliable, positive big picture and plenty of feedback that said they [the investors and potential partners] were on the right track."

No investor told Archbold they'd accept 1,000 bits of progress as a substitute for a positive P&L. No potential partner stated they'd sign on if they saw 1,000 hints of gathering momentum. But Archbold intuitively knew how investors and partners would view that information. He put himself in the stakeholder's shoes and used his head to empathize. The result was a brilliant plan that saved the company from going under.

USE YOUR HEART

John Mantello was an executive with an Asian auto manufacturer when he first truly understood the impact his heart played in creating empathy.

"I had always believed empathy was about being customer-oriented," he said. "You know, being polite and professional, looking to strike a win/win agreement with a client. Before I joined the auto manufacturer, I was a reasonably successful car dealer and had many solid customer relationships with both consumers and other dealers. I thought my ability to empathize was quite good."

But then Mantello had an experience that made him realize that his empathy was just idling in the background until he really engaged his heart with his head.

My company sold a line of new cars that retailed for the price of an average used car. That made our product very popular with many first-time buyers and value-conscious shoppers, providing dealers with a lot of traffic and great word of mouth.

Some of our dealers liked the traffic but saw our customers as price shoppers. They treated them professionally but reservedly—like all the customer really wanted was to grind the dealer down for the lowest price.

It was about noon on a drizzly Wednesday in autumn. I was visiting one of my dealers at his downtown location.

As I walked the lot with the dealer principal, I saw a young man and woman huddled together under the canopy trying to stay dry. I asked my client, "What are they waiting for?"

"That's our new car pickup area. They are here to get the car they bought on Sunday. It took them a while to get their credit done," the dealer said with a tone that told me he believed these were two of those typical price shoppers.

I looked more closely. The woman was obviously with her boyfriend or fiancé (I saw no wedding ring). She glanced at him with that unmistakable "he's the one" look as she held his hand.

Then I peeked at her partner. His eyes were surveying the

lot anticipating this new car, the first major purchase in their life together.

Suddenly, I thought back to my wife, Anne, and our first big splurge, a dining table and chairs for our small flat. There were so many emotions that the table symbolized. My heart took over my thinking as I connected my memories of Anne and me with the situation on the lot.

These two weren't just buying a value-priced small car, I thought, this was the first of the many major commitments they'd share. I imagined the pride he had in being able to get his first financing and the future she imagined this car symbolized. I was overwhelmed with the emotions of the moment—how they were feeling and what they must be thinking.

Because of this increased empathy, Mantello didn't even have to talk to the couple under the canopy to be aware of what they really wanted. Their body language and a few physical clues (like no wedding ring) combined with his own memories of what it was like to be part of a young couple told him everything. His mind filled with thoughts about the pair's likely expectations and what could be done to satisfy them.

I wondered, had the salesman or general manager connected with any of this? Sure they sold the customer, but had they made enough of a connection to sell any aftermarket services or to even be sure that the customer came back for service and for their next car? Most dealers don't, and that's why the business has so much trouble turning a fair profit.

So I asked them if they thought about the couple's situation and their likely feelings (even though I instinctively knew the answer). They just looked at me like I was speaking another language. They hadn't seen anything more than a cute young gal and her scruffy boyfriend—a pair of twenty-somethings with questionable credit looking to score the lowest price in town.

Mantello realized that this level of empathetic connection enabled him to understand a lot more about that couple than the dealer or the salesman. That understanding prepared him to negotiate their satisfaction far better than someone (like the dealer) who saw them as price shoppers.

Since that day two years ago, Mantello has taught automobile sales managers and salespeople to use their hearts and see the products and services they offer through their clients' eyes. As a result, they have seen better gross profits and customer sell rates. And before long, they expect to see the difference empathy makes in their customer-retention rates, a critical component for long-term profitability in the car business.

HAVE COURAGE

Acting on empathetic instincts requires a lot of courage. Why? Because you're acting on your intuitions instead of relying on facts and figures or concrete proof before you make a move. It took a lot of guts for Guy Archbold to invent a strategy of using "virtual sales" to secure more partners and investors. And when John Mantello started to teach the role empathy plays in a profitable auto business, he needed guts to face hard-core auto sellers who thought, "He's lost it."

Coraine realized that the secret to developing more empathy among managers at Union Square Hospitality Group is feedback. "You need to empower someone to hold the mirror up to you so you can see how well you are connecting. That probably takes more courage than any other part [of the recipe for empathy]. You have to find someone whose insights you trust [or are willing to trust] wholeheartedly," Coraine says. "You really have to want to improve and welcome their feedback."

Coraine requires that all managers get feedback on their level of empathy. "We *all* have someone who holds the mirror up to us," he explains, meaning even the top executives open themselves to critique. "People gravitate toward what the boss shows is important, so that challenge [to work on empathy] goes right up the tree."

Coraine's coach is a woman who is his subordinate on the organizational chart. "My associate Hannah Kluger has the most incredible instincts," he said. "She picks up subtle signals, sees what's going on inside of people, and never misses. She has helped me in all my dealings. I give her the license to be frank about me and everybody around us. She plays a huge role in my success."

Coraine believes everybody who wants to grow their capacity for empathy needs someone like Hannah to watch over them as they interact with others. He has developed a list of things this "empathy coach" should watch for and report on, the signs that someone is not using their head and their heart when interacting with customers, coworkers, bosses, and others. They tend to:

- Not respond to what the other person has said
- Abruptly change the topic
- Become noticeably bored
- Focus on what was said, rather than why
- Show that they thought what was said was trivial or unimportant
- Not be emotionally present
- Decline to give useful feedback

Another important act of courage, Coraine believes, is for managers to clear their organizations of anyone who might "skunk" people who use their empathy and make intuitive choices about expectations.

By "skunk" Coraine means associates or bosses who "spray negativity and then run off. Skunks spray when they feel threatened," he noted. "Associates or bosses who feel threatened, are having a bad day, or are just being unthinking and uncaring in that moment all have the potential to be a skunk."

If the young woman at the hotel who had taken Coraine's order for chicken soup and crackers had been told by the chef, "Let him wait like everybody else!" when she requested the order be fulfilled quickly, that would be skunking her.

This is how the empathy effect is lost in many organizations. People come to their jobs with a spark, and instead of it getting fanned into a fire someone douses them with negativity, extinguishing their initiative.

At the Union Square Hospitality Group, they have a "no skunk-ing" policy. It's enforced by the employees and backed up by Coraine personally.

Many of the managers I interviewed have used their ability to read between the lines to great advantage. It was his intuition that helped Bill Zollars know what Yellow's truck drivers and depot per-sonnel expected when he was lining up support for his big multi-million-dollar transformation initiative. The same kind of instinct helped Joanne Lipman get everyone at the *Wall Street Journal* to follow through in the paper's redesign.

But when these executives were asked how they developed and refined their ability to read between the lines with bosses, associ-ates, and customers, none could explain their methods. The best answer came from Yellow CEO Bill Zollars. "You have to *want* to do it," he advised.

That helps a little. The reason most people miss signals is that they don't make reading between the lines a priority. It takes a lot of energy and focus. But it also takes specific discipline.

Richard Coraine has found the recipe for empathy. It's one part smarts, one part heart, and a dollop of courage. Try it. You'll be amazed at the effect it has on your ability to read between the lines.

3 MORE ACCURATE ASSESSMENTS

H er expectations couldn't have been any clearer.

Yet after five years of what everyone thought was effective follow-through, the CEO of a $1.8-billion health care system realized all her organization had done was, in her words, a lot of "mucking around."

"One of our senior people came back from a hospital visit," Sister Mary Jean Ryan, the CEO of SSM Health Care, explained. "While he was on-site, an associate asked him, 'Are we still doing *CQI?*'" (CQI was the continuous-quality-improvement initiative they had introduced five years earlier.)

"When I heard that," Ryan admitted, "I almost collapsed."

Despite giving her leadership team the crystal-clear goal of getting CQI up and working in every hospital along with loads of resources, SSM Health Care hadn't followed through. In fact, their deployment of CQI was so hit-and-miss that front-line associates were left wondering if headquarters was serious about the program.

Facing such a stinging indictment of an organization's ability to follow through, the average executive looks for an excuse. "This stuff might work great at other companies," is the typical rationalization, "but we're different. Nobody in our industry [or our size or in our locale] has gotten it to work. We'd better try something else."

But Ryan and her team are not at all average. They didn't make lame excuses or blame other people. They stared this significant waste of time and effort in the face and forced themselves to make an accurate assessment. "We knew this [CQI] was right," Ryan said. "It had to be something *we* were missing."

Ryan's team looked below the surface to find the root cause of their missteps (a key component of making more accurate assessments). That's how they discovered the cause of their lack of follow-through: SSM's managers had jumped from deciding what they wanted to do, to doing it, without really thinking it through.

They hadn't precisely plotted their starting point, or thoroughly evaluated the challenges they were likely to face. Leadership was overconfident, assuming they knew much more than they did. They didn't test their confidence by comparing the gaps between what they expected to happen and what was really happening on the front lines during the critical first few steps of CQI deployment.

As a result, they didn't have a clear direction. And they spent five years accomplishing next to nothing.

Once they made this candid assessment, other—more thorough—evaluations followed and a clear direction crystallized quickly. Ryan and her team went back to following through, making more accurate assessments to be sure they stayed on track. "The second year into our [renewed] program, we could see we were on the cusp," Ryan said.

Over the next two years, SSM Health Care was able to get CQI processes deployed in several of the system's hospitals. Their follow-through was so good that several member hospitals were recognized as the best in Oklahoma, Missouri, Illinois, and Wisconsin's (their home states) annual review of firms implementing CQI programs.

Then, in 2002, SSMHC became the first-ever winner in the newly created health care category of the Malcolm Baldrige

National Quality Award. (Baldrige is an evaluation and awards program for companies practicing CQI, run by the National Institute of Standards and Technology.)

SSMHC's thirteen-year odyssey—beginning with the clearest of expectations, followed by five years of mucking around, before learning to make more accurate assessments and seeing deployment take off like a rocket—is a graphic example of what it takes to set and maintain a clear direction.

Clear expectations are not enough. Clear direction requires a comprehensive system for assessing how you are doing at each step of the way.

MUCKING AROUND IS COMMON

According to a one-of-a-kind study, organizations both public and private end up "mucking around" (spending significant time and effort without getting anywhere near their goal) in one out of every two initiatives they take on.

Researchers from Ohio State's Fisher College of Business studied hundreds of decisions in marketing, purchasing, product development, human resources, and manufacturing.* They watched as managers recognized the need for changes and continued monitoring as leadership gathered the facts, mulled over their options, and set their decisions in motion. The scholars then graded each organization using just one measure: Did they follow through for at least twenty-four months, or did their initiative slip through the cracks?

Here's their bleak conclusion:

Half of all the time and effort management invests in a program to solve some problem or take advantage of an opportunity will be wasted.

What's the cause of all that wasted time and effort? Dr. Paul C. Nutt, author of the study, concluded it was the way managers made

*Dr. Paul C. Nutt, "Surprising but True: Half the Decisions in Organizations Fail," Academy of Management Executive, Vol. 14, No. 4, 1999.

their assessments of where they were, what to do, and how to do it that was at the root of their problem.

"[Decision-making] tactics prone to fail were used in two out of every three decisions that were studied," Dr. Nutt wrote. In his 2002 book *Why Decisions Fail,* Dr. Nutt detailed twenty-one separate categories of flawed decision-making tactics—from failing to look below the surface and jumping to conclusions to letting personal emotions cloud a business judgment. Each, the professor concluded, was the result of not using a *system* for making sure managers were asking themselves the right questions and generating accurate answers before taking action.

Why do so many managers fail to notice this gaping hole in their decision-making processes? One of the biggest reasons is that very few organizations keep track of when their assessments prove accurate and when they don't.

"Managers can recall their successes and failures," Nutt wrote, "but seldom subject them to systematic analysis."

In fact, despite all the computer power and data warehousing in a modern enterprise, another study found, fewer than one out of ten American organizations track the quality of their thinking.

"You would think organizations would be keeping and sharing information on how successful decisions were made—in order to replicate them—and how bad decisions were arrived at—in order to learn from their mistakes," a research team from Kepner Tregoe wrote in a report titled "Decision Making in the Digital Age." But in a survey of more than a thousand executives, nine out of ten managers (90 percent) said their organizations don't capture that information or provide managers with a discipline for making more accurate assessments.

As a result, Nutt notes, managers make "erroneous associations between the tactics and their results . . . and continue using [tactics] with poor track records."

Imagine the advantage you would have if you turned those terrible statistics around in your business? The lessons of SSM Health Care will show you how.

MAKING MORE ACCURATE ASSESSMENTS

When I first told an associate (I'll call him Jay) from the telecommunications giant Sprint that a Baldrige National Award for Quality winner had instituted a comprehensive system for making more accurate assessments, he was cynical.

"We use the Baldrige criteria [here at Sprint] and train much like Baldrige examiners," this insider reported. "It hasn't produced anything close to more accurate assessments.

"I've seen the applications we do [the list of Baldrige questions and Sprint's answers]. It all sounds very good, but *I know* we don't evaluate employees or do our work that way."

The Baldrige National Quality Program (at www.quality.nist.gov) is a part of the National Institute of Standards and Technology. The agency is devoted to helping businesses improve their competitive advantage through continuous quality improvement. They have established a series of questions—about leadership systems, strategic direction, customer expectations, measurement systems, employee training and development, and operations and performance metrics—to help companies evaluate their quality-improvement programs. But as Jay realized, knowing the right questions to ask and making accurate assessments are two different things.

That's why this chapter isn't about the Baldrige questions or the processes of companies practicing continuous improvement. Instead, I try to explain what Jay didn't know: Beneath the Baldrige criteria are three *connected* disciplines that assure more accurate assessments for any company implementing an initiative. The story of SSM Health Care shows that if you use all three, you're guaranteed to come up with a clear direction and avoid "mucking around."

Discipline One—Put It in Writing

Discipline Two—Look Below the Surface

Discipline Three—Let Someone Else Check Your Accuracy

Discipline One: Put It in Writing

"We have a tradition [in business] of managers getting together and planning," Dr. William Starbuck explained, "going to a conference room and deciding, 'What shall we do to make more money?' or 'How shall we market this new product?' The assumption is . . . pooled judgments [from the managers in the meeting] provide an adequate basis for [accurate] decision making."

Starbuck is a professor of management from NYU's Stern School of Business. He has studied the above scenario (that a bunch of managers sitting around talking is a sound method for making business decisions) and concluded *it's based on a dangerous assumption.*

"Managers often have badly distorted pictures of their businesses and their environments," the professor wrote in his 2003 report on the accuracy of managers' perceptions.*

In other words, what's been whispered around many corporate water coolers is true: Most managers know a lot less than they think. In fact, according to the professor's research, six out of ten managers in a meeting are likely to be seriously out of touch. With all those inaccurate perceptions polluting the group's assessments, it's no wonder organizations spend half their time spinning their wheels.

Starbuck and his coauthor, John Mezias, listed many of the factors that cause so many managers to be out of touch, including:
- "Many top managers surround themselves with yes-sayers," claim Starbuck and Mezias. "[These yes-sayers] filter out signs of trouble and warnings from middle managers." So managers at the top "see fewer, milder deficiencies" than actually exist.
- Other execs' "interpersonal skills and demeanor encourage colleagues and subordinates to . . . conceal or dissimulate [hide the straight answers to tough questions]." Once again, managers stay blissfully unaware and make inaccurate assessments of what's happening at work.

*John M. Mezias and William H. Starbuck, "Studying the Accuracy of Managers' Perceptions: A Research Odyssey," *British Journal of Management*, Vol. 14, 3–17, 2003.

- Managers let their faulty memories, most recent personal observations, water cooler chitchat, news articles, management gurus, and other unreliable sources dominate their assessments instead of skeptically reviewing all the alleged facts.
- Most managers have a tendency to leap to conclusions, seek confirmatory evidence [the facts that tell them they are right] while ignoring disconfirming evidence, and are overconfident about the validity of their judgments.

Starbuck's and Mezias's research suggests that leadership needs to do something to make sure that managers bring more accurate assessments to their decision making. They make two specific suggestions:

1. When organizations base decisions and strategies on managers' perceptions, they need to draw data from the managers who have a record of greater accuracy, while discarding data from the rest.

2. To stop the flow of inaccurate data, executives need to "encourage managers to admit their errors and to modify their approach accordingly."

How can an organization separate the good thinking from the bad? What could they do to encourage participants to be more careful about their stated opinions and modify their thinking process? Those questions raise some touchy subjects. Most sensible managers (especially politically adept middle managers) wouldn't touch that subject with a ten-foot pole.

But they don't need to. It is possible to improve in-house accuracy without voicing a word of criticism. Just make it a policy that when making important decisions everyone must *put their thoughts in writing*.

Writing things down—whether it's the answer to a problem, a response to a question, or an opinion on the current state of the market—stops any manager in his tracks. He or she realizes without being told that, "Hey, people are going to read this and judge me and my capabilities. I'd better be more careful, thorough, and accurate." Writing forces people to be more aware about what they know and what they don't know, and can help them see when they aren't thinking things through thoroughly.

When you write, the holes in your logic are more apparent. Each flaw—a vague expectation, a hasty conclusion, or a failure of common sense or just plain ignorance—is easier for you (and others) to notice.

Written reports also create a permanent record, so that any conclusions can be compared and graded for accuracy. After a few rounds, every manager's input can be given the weight it deserves, allowing executives to draw on assessments from the more accurate managers and discard the input from those who are less careful and more unreliable.

SSM PUT IT IN WRITING

SSMIIC saw the benefits of putting more things in writing almost immediately.

"For example," Ryan said, "the Baldrige application had a question that asked us to describe our leadership system.

"I didn't have a clue what that meant, what a *leadership system* was."

When most managers are asked questions they don't know the answer to, many, according to Starbuck and Mezias, "seem to be content to fill in the gaps with folklore." In other words, they make stuff up, or repeat some jargon that's supposed to sound knowledgeable but on closer inspection actually says nothing. But managers tend not to make that mistake twice if they have to put their answers in writing to be shared with their peers and made part of the permanent record.

See for yourself. Ask an executive to describe their ideal leadership system. Most will take a crack at it, verbally, right then and there. But if you ask the same manager to give you that answer in writing, they'll want time to do some homework first and draft several versions before they hand it back to you for your review. (One manager recently told me he spent three weeks writing and rewriting a simple two-page introduction of his business unit for new associates.)

At SSMHC, writing turned out to be an incredibly powerful force for setting a clear direction. For example, the Baldrige criteria asked SSMHC executives to write their response to the standard question "How do you convey the mission of the organization?" According to Ryan, writing that answer changed everything about the way the team followed through on their mission statement.

CREATING A MISSION STATEMENT THAT ISN'T A CROCK

"We had collected twenty-one single-spaced pages of [suggested] mission and values statements from [employees] around the system . . . twenty-one pages!" Ryan said. "So when the Baldrige process asked us how we convey the values and mission," Ryan said with a laugh, "we all asked, 'Which one?'"

The inability to compose an accurate response to that question compelled Ryan and her team to generate a *single* statement that could be shared by every employee and associated physician. After months of getting input from thousands of associates, then writing, reviewing, and rewriting, Ryan and her team settled on thirteen words that encapsulated their shared purpose: "Through our exceptional heath care services we reveal the healing presence of God."

Ryan was enormously proud of their accomplishment. "We got to those thirteen words through the active participation of over 3,000 committed employees," she said.

But as soon as they read what they had written, Ryan and her top managers realized that their statement begged for greater clarification. "Anybody can say they're exceptional," Ryan told her executive team. "We need to define it so we can measure it."

So the team found the five characteristics that defined "exceptional" for their health care system: exceptional clinical outcomes; exceptional patient, employee, and physician satisfaction; and exceptional financial results.

Once the characteristics were in writing, the team saw they

needed to define each one further so that it could be measured—for example, providing an exceptional clinical outcome could include having a very low unplanned-readmittance rate; and exceptional patient satisfaction could include receiving high marks from patients for pain management. Each of the five characteristics was detailed in full so that every single employee could see how well their unit was contributing to the mission.

After writing the mission statement in plain English and defining it, management recognized that each employee and department needed to share it. Company leaders needed to guide the day-to-day efforts of the workforce so that the mission statement wouldn't be the typical empty directive that shows up on the masthead of the company newsletter.

That led SSMHC to cascade their mission to every level of their organization. For example, a department might say that they would improve patient satisfaction (part of being exceptional) that year by X percent by reducing the time it takes to respond to a patient's call for assistance to five minutes. Then they'd use a chart to track their progress. A similar process was performed on all of the five "exceptional" characteristics—in clinical outcomes; patient, employee, and physician satisfaction; and financial results. To complete the process, management set systemwide targets for the following three years and distributed them to each department of each hospital, including all 23,000 employees.

So by the time Ryan and her team were done writing their answer to that one question, "What are your values and mission?" each and every employee could describe and track how he or she contributed to the mission every single day.

"We learned it [having a mission] takes more than inspirational themes and clever communications," Ryan stated. Writing everything down caused Ryan and her team to define their mission so they could measure it, make it real for every employee, and then track the implementation so every day every associate can see how they are sharing in the purpose—"Through our exceptional health care services we reveal the healing presence of God."

By *putting it in writing,* SSM Health Care is now one of the few companies on the planet whose mission statement won't be seen by employees and customers as a lot of hot air.

Discipline Two: Look Below the Surface

"As you identify a problem," Ryan explained, "it's not enough to say, 'I think it's this or that . . .' You have to go back and follow the process until you find the roots of the problem."

Looking below the surface is the second discipline for making more accurate assessments. In order to avoid a project's becoming the one out of every two initiatives that fail, managers need to take the time to examine the layers of a problem or situation that are not obvious or apparent.

"[Taking the time to look below the surface] was a different approach for us," noted William Thompson, the senior VP for strategic development at SSMHC. "In health care we typically would identify a problem and immediately jump to a solution.

"Say we were trying to improve start times for surgery. Originally, we would get some supervisors together and they would decide 'It's probably anesthesia's fault.' Then they'd assign somebody to fix anesthesia.

"Six months later, after making changes in anesthesia, we'd discover we still hadn't fixed the problem. And we'd get together again and take another stab at reducing late surgical starts."

This is a very common scenario in organizations big and small. Managers are under the gun. Three out of four of them are making more decisions per day than they were just five years ago. Nobody has a longer day than five years ago, so those managers are making their decisions with less time. It's not surprising that managers would jump to conclusions in order to save some time.

But you're not saving time if you have to revisit a problem in six months and work out another solution. (Again, if businesses were keeping track of their follow-through and noting the paths that caused them to fail, this incredible drag on productivity would be more obvious.)

The discipline of looking below the surface and linking cause and effect changed SSMHC's tendency to jump to conclusions. "Now we realize we were failing because we hadn't identified the root cause of late surgical starts. Was it: Late surgeons? Improper equipment? Testing? Scheduling snafus? Anesthesia? Or something else?" Thompson said.

Looking below the surface, SSMHC learned, is a four-part process:

1. **Brainstorm all the potential causes using front-line experts.** SSMHC starts their analysis of any problem by assembling a team of people who are intimately familiar with the situation, instead of looking to executives far removed from the front lines. "For surgical starts [the scheduled time for surgery to begin], we'd get surgical nurses, scrub nurses, techs, and surgeons—everyone who's close to the O.R.," Thompson explained. "The ideal team has five to eight participants (not including any management from headquarters, although they can sit in). The group will take the time to look at possible direct and indirect causes of a late surgical start and then, from that list, pick out both likely and seemingly unlikely causes. The idea is to get a comprehensive list of possibilities and potentially uncover a previously ignored but influential cause."

2. **Narrow possible causes down, by group vote, to three or four most likely.** After the team creates their long (and often messy) list of ten to fifty possibilities, the group edits the list to choose the ones that need closer review. The group vote is important. Every participant comes to a problem with preconceived notions and personal prejudices, which could cause them to weigh possibilities inaccurately. Group voting circumvents any hidden agendas and blind spots.

3. **Collect data and test for the linkage.** Contrary to what some may think, this does not need to be a big, expensive research project. Teams at SSMHC use commonsense approaches to deciding if their possible causes are the right ones. "We might create a log," Thompson said, "with a simple checklist of the causes." Then, for two weeks or a month, a designated person would note

when a surgery started late and immediately check the cause of the late start from a checklist of four possibilities. The group would then collect the data and tally the different causes. The one with the most checkmarks as the root cause would get more scrutiny. Again, this discipline eliminates perceptual inaccuracy as it eliminates reliance on a manager's memory.

4. **Come up with a solution.** Once the "root-cause teams" at SSMHC have brainstormed a wide range of potential causes, narrowed them down using their front-line expertise, and tested the top three or four possibilities at the source using commonsense data, the group is ready to fix the problem. According to Thompson, the participants then get back together again, and are then much more effective at finding a lasting solution.

Accurate assessments are not simply a matter of experience, credentials, or position in the hierarchy. To offset management's documented tendency to jump to conclusions, confront every problem with the discipline to look below the surface and uncover the root causes.

A S K   " W H Y ? "   F I V E   T I M E S

One of the simplest methods for looking below the surface is called The Five Whys. Taiichi Ohno, creator of the Toyota Production System and a pioneer in continuous quality movement, believed that if managers wanted to start with a clear and accurate assessment of any company problem, they had to ask and answer "Why?" five times before trying to create a solution.

At SSMHC, those five whys might have gone something like this:

"Why were we 'mucking around' for five years?"

Answer: The company's continuous-quality-improvement projects weren't tied into the strategic goals of each operating unit. (This is just one of the possible answers. When using The Five Whys, you must take every answer individually and follow it to its root.)

"Why weren't the projects tied to the unit's strategic goals?"

Answer: It wasn't a criterion for selecting projects.

"Why wasn't this a criterion?"

Answer: We didn't know it was important.

"Why didn't we know what was important?"

Answer: We hadn't asked ourselves the right questions at the start to tell us what was important and what wasn't.

"Why didn't we ask the right questions?"

Answer: We didn't know what questions to ask.

Using The Five Whys, SSM could have avoided five years of failed follow-through. They would have realized that the root cause of their wasted time and effort was not knowing the right questions to ask.

This simple discipline has an incredible power to reveal what you're doing wrong. Try it the next time you have a problem.

Discipline Three: Let Someone Else Check Your Accuracy

According to Harry Hertz, the director of the Baldrige National Quality Program, some 250,000 managers download assessment and information tools from the Baldrige Web site every month. Yet, in any given year, fewer than one hundred organizations will apply for the award. Why do so few organizations apply? Some know they are not ready; others may not be motivated enough. But many are likely to be put off by the third element in the Baldrige disciplines, which is to *open up* completely to a team of outsiders who will come in and check to see that the company actually does what it says it does.

The average American tells 2,555 white lies a year, about seven every day. At work those white lies turn into spin. Managers are skilled at spinning themselves and using their power and position to compel others to play along. The only way around this tendency is to know that at some point somebody is going to look and report on whether you are being completely accurate.

Every Baldrige award application triggers a site visit. It's like an annual physical where a company, instead of a patient, strips to let a doctor check for any signs of ill health or disease. Those examiners turn the lights up bright, exposing everything about the applicant. (At SSM Health Care, more than eight hundred employees at every level and physicians from throughout the system were interviewed to check on the accuracy of the sixty-three pages of written answers on their application.)

"People [managers] inside have a set of blinders," Baldrige judge Joseph Muzikowski said. "They need an outsider to hold up the mirror." Muzikowski, the VP of Business Process and Strategic Supply for Solvay America, started as a Baldrige examiner and later became a judge. He's covered more than sixty in-depth examinations during his time with the foundation.

"They [the examiners] will dig down into the dirt and mud and look at the linkages. The key issue for Baldrige is Does this all [the words on the application and the evidence gathered in the site visit] fit together?" said Muzikowski. "For instance, you look at how they listen and learn from customers. If the customer says, 'I need something done in seven days,' and your process takes ten, we want to know what you are doing to find that gap and close it."

Do you recall what Jay (the engineer from Sprint) said at the opening of this chapter? "We did [written] applications," Jay said. "[But when] you look at what they [the executive team] have written, you say, 'We don't evaluate employees that way. That task doesn't get done that way. I *know* it doesn't work that way.'"

Without exposing themselves to knowledgeable and *uncompromised* individuals, Sprint's Baldrige-style assessment process was bound to be inaccurate. As the world has learned from the epidemic of financial fraud among companies audited by the big five accountancies, it's not enough to hire someone to check the accuracy of internal practices. They need to be uncompromised.

It doesn't have to be an outsider. At Sprint the reviews could have come from a team of straight-talking lower-level employees, like Jay. The emperor, if you remember the famous story, needed only a single innocent child to find out he had no clothes.

YELLOW CHECKS THEIR ACCURACY

Bill Zollars, CEO of the parent company of Yellow Transportation (Yellow Roadway Corporation), wanted the logistics company to start exceeding customers' expectations by making sure their clients were *very* satisfied (instead of just satisfied) with the company's services. So Zollars asked Yellow Transportation's then marketing chief about the company's level of customer satisfaction. "What do our customers think of us?" he inquired.

"They like us" was the VP of Marketing's assessment.

The average executive would feel pretty comfortable with this off-the-cuff assessment. After all, Yellow wasn't failing—thousands of customers called for their services every day. Zollars saw no obvious signals of dissatisfaction—no massive complaints, no big client defections, or even a survey that said the average customer didn't "like" them. "Our customers like us" seemed like a perfectly reasonable conclusion. "Okay," the average senior executive might have thought, "we're starting at *like* and we need a program to move the needle from *like* to *like a lot*."

But Zollars is another above-average manager. He decided to check to be absolutely sure his VP had made an accurate assessment of Yellow's customer satisfaction.

Zollars assigned a team of executives to roll up their sleeves and dig into boxes of recent client transactions. "Find out," he told the team, "did we do what we were asked to do?" His thinking was that if someone pays you to do something and you don't do it, they can't really *like* you. A couple boxes of transactions would give him a sense of Yellow's track record.

Zollars learned very quickly that his VP was way, way off. In four out of every ten transactions, Yellow had failed in one or more of the three fundamental expectations customers have of a logistics services company (to be on time, to keep things intact, and to write an accurate bill). "How on earth could the VP say customers like us?" Zollars asked himself. "We let them down almost half of the time."

Had Zollars gone with his VP of Marketing's opinion, there's no telling how much more mucking around his company would have done. Instead, by checking the accuracy of customer sentiments, he discovered that Yellow first needed to stop disappointing those four out of ten customers. Once that first step was accomplished, Zollars and his executives could begin an initiative to take Yellow's clients from "satisfied" to "thrilled."

Yellow followed through quickly, curing all the causes of client disappointment. They soon reduced their defect rate from 40 percent to under 4 percent, earning Yellow a number one in customer service ranking from *Logistics Management* magazine's annual "Quest for Quality." Zollars had checked the accuracy of his manager's perceptions, and that made all the difference.

IS ACCURACY TOO MUCH TO ASK FOR?

Professor William Starbuck, coauthor of *Studying the Accuracy of Managers' Perceptions*, thought Sister Mary Jean Ryan represented a one-of-a-kind CEO. "The case you're studying is not transferable," he said, "because of the culture of the nuns. They have a dedication to be truthful. They live in an environment where they are truthful with each other. They are better able to deal with the truth than most of us are."

More typical CEOs are so tied up in being seen as right, they cover up all errors and misjudgments. Starbuck spoke of another big-company CEO that he met during his research. "He [the boss] knew exactly how things were and that they were perfect," Starbuck said ironically. "No way *he* wanted to make [or hear about] any changes." Ryan's willingness to allow herself to see the unvarnished truth was atypical in Starbuck's opinion. He connected that trait to Ryan's religious affiliation.

Ryan *is* very open to facing the unvarnished truth. However, believing that's due to her connection with the Franciscan Sisters of Mary is a big assumption, one that jumps past a lot of possible answers to reach its conclusion. There are certainly many other organizations and managers just as open as Ryan (like Zollars and many others featured throughout this book). But Starbuck's concern raises an important point.

You can't trust the good character of the manager when you need clear and accurate assessments. Everyone has to know that there will be an audit process.

As the nineteenth-century social philosopher Jeremy Bentham wrote, "The more strictly we are watched, the better we behave." It's only by letting others check our accuracy that we give ourselves the impetus to make more accurate assessments.

Building Block II

■

THE RIGHT PEOPLE

Now that you have the means to create a clear direction, you're probably anxious to get started immediately. You wouldn't be alone. Sister Mary Jean Ryan, the CEO of SSMHC (introduced in the last building block), admits she's often felt that urge. "I was taught if you can't fix something overnight, well . . . what good are you?" she said.

But the research out of Ohio State's Fisher College of Business is conclusive*—managers who make sure they have the right fit between their people and goals *before* they take action double the likelihood of successful follow-through. That's more than a 100 percent increase in successful follow-through for simply fitting the right people to your goals. "Always match resources to outcomes" is how military strategists have defined this critical step for avoiding mission failure.

In the next three chapters, you'll learn how to match your people with your outcomes. You'll read fresh tactics for finding the *right*

*Dr. Paul C. Nutt, "Surprising but True: Half the Decisions in Organizations Fail," *Academy of Management Executive*, Vol. 14, No. 4, 1999.

associates for your team, and how to make sure that everyone's on the *same page*. Last, we'll upend the conventional wisdom about what it takes to manage follow-through, and discover how to find the right person to take the lead in every initiative.

4 HIRE ATTITUDES OVER EXPERIENCE

How do you decide what sort of person is right for your team? If you ask the average human resources manager that question, you'll find he's probably working on an unspoken assumption—the candidate's experience should match your job specs as closely as possible. HR has been trained to think that employee selection is like finding a key for a lock—an exact fit opens the door to top performance. And for them that exact fit is found by comparing a candidate's résumé to the knowledge, abilities, and skills the job requires.

In other words, to decide what sort of person is right for your team, conventional HR wisdom looks for a candidate who's already done what you're doing. If you can't find an exact fit, the wisdom continues, you should get as close as possible to a precise experience match.

Hiring for experience should suit your follow-through just fine if:
- You're in a business where today is a lot like yesterday
- When something changes there's no rush to change with it
- You can count on other companies to weed out employees with

serious performance flaws (like making bad decisions under pressure or pointing fingers when things don't go as planned) before they make it to *your* doorstep

But if your business is constantly changing, or if it's important that your people adapt quickly to new ideas, or if you've hired for experience only to learn that the person you hired didn't fit in with your team or your company culture, you need to use another criterion than past perfomance. As you'll see in this chapter, a number of successful leaders and managers feel that hiring for the right attitudes assures a much better fit than hiring for the right experience.

In this chapter I'll show you when the right attitudes outweigh experience, how to determine what attitudes fit *your* team and *your* goals, and how to screen for candidates who will make the best fit.

ATTITUDES OR EXPERIENCE?

The new federal goods and services tax looked like it was going to be a nightmare for millions of business executives. The forms were confusing and compliance was complicated. So the national tax chief promised executives he'd create a toll-free telephone support line where management and their staff could get help.

John was the department head assigned to staff and manage this new government service. He was given a budget, some office space, and a memo from the tax office's human resources department outlining the proper credentials to look for when screening applicants.

But John didn't think a two-year accounting degree or three years of tax experience would guarantee he would get the kind of people who could handle the pressure of a new program and lots of irritable callers. His gut told him the right attitudes were more important. So he ignored the recommended guidelines and conducted scores of unorthodox interviews—asking questions to uncover the applicant's attitudes. He focused on finding someone who was willing and able to be inventive and stay calm under pressure, rather than experienced with tax forms.

The other department heads thought John was making a terrible career decision. They told him that when you work for the government, you should follow the advice of the senior bureaucrats to the letter. That way if something goes wrong, you're off the hook.

But John ignored their warnings. He hired an eclectic crew who had less "official" experience but were more conscientious and better problem-solvers than the rest of the applicant pool.

As the tax deadline approached and the first round of calls streamed in, John's staff was stymied. Their database didn't include the right answers to many critical questions. John realized it would take more time to get all the data his people needed on-line, and that delay would cause an uproar from the businesspeople he was supposed to help. He started to have second thoughts. "Maybe the other department heads were right," John said to himself. "This help desk might be a no-win situation."

But his fears evaporated quickly as his staff took charge of the situation. "I rang you tax guys with a question and you didn't have an answer," said one gruff business executive when he reached John's direct line. "So your people went home, found the information on the Internet, and followed through with me the next day! *Who are you guys really?*"

The staff had taken it upon themselves to fill the holes in the database and show their "customer" he was in good hands. This happened time and time again. John's staff's bedside manner was so good that, as he put it, "people couldn't believe they were talking to civil servants in the federal tax office."

The taxpayer help desk was a huge success. While the tax stayed unpopular, legislators called to congratulate the national commissioner. John was a hero within the agency.

Within a year, John was being invited to address other government and nongovernment people to share his experience in hiring attitudes over experience. Today his biggest worry is how he'll keep those doubting department heads from stealing his "inexperienced" staff.

HOW TO DECIDE WHAT YOU NEED

John knew instinctively that his taxpayer support line would do better if he hired the right attitudes instead of the right experience. His instincts were in line with what managers from Microsoft (who screen for intelligence over experience), Southwest Airlines (who look for character and team chemistry), and the new president of Harvard University (who has directed his deans to look for *promise* over past accomplishments when they decide who should get tenure).

There's a short list of questions that will help assess how important the right attitudes are to follow-through. Consider each in deciding if you should give greater weight to attitudes or to experience in your hiring process.

1. **Does the job call for a lot of problem solving?** Are associates expected to fill in the gaps between company procedures and what situations demand? Do customers look to you for solutions to unique problems or ask you to tailor the standard offers to their needs? Does your company expect employees to participate in continuous-quality-improvement programs? How important is it to balance intuitive leaps, logical analysis, and realistic assessments in this job? Rate your need for a creative problem-solver.

   Follow the process manual   *Innovate and create solutions*

1	2	3	4	5	6	7

2. **Will your staff have a lot of autonomy?** How much supervision will employees have? Will someone show them the ropes, or do you expect them to find their own answers? Rate your requirements for individual initiative.

   Structured environment   *You're on your own*

1	2	3	4	5	6	7

3. **Must the associate handle frustration and uncertainty really well?** How unpredictable is the work environment? How often will this employee be asked to handle unpleasant tasks? Are there a lot of job-related tensions, like headquarters moving the goalposts after the budgets are set? Is this employee expected to effectively deal with upset and disap-

pointment caused by others out of your control? Rate your requirements for levelheadedness and coping mechanisms.

OK for average breaking point   *Needs extra maturity*

   1   2   3   4   5   6   7

4. **Are the things they're able to learn on the job more important than the things they bring to the job?** How volatile is your competitive environment? How many things have changed unpredictably in the last few years? Do you expect this person to take on and grow into new responsibilities? Determine your need for someone who can learn more and adapt constantly.

Routine, predictable work   *Lots of change*

   1   2   3   4   5   6   7

5. **How important is teamwork?** Do your people need to collaborate and coordinate? Do you need people who work out their conflicts among themselves? Does your staff depend on others outside your control to get things done? Rate the importance of being agreeable and able to network.

Individual performance   *Total teamwork*

   1   2   3   4   5   6   7

6. **Have you lost good people because they "don't fit in"?** How rigid is your corporate culture? Do you have "hot buttons" that can set you off? Does your boss? Have your associates forced someone out? How important is personal chemistry?

We'll adjust   *Needs to fit the culture*

   1   2   3   4   5   6   7

In general, the higher you score a position for problem-solving, autonomy, learning ability, interpersonal skills, team chemistry, etc., the more important it is that you find candidates with the right attitudes.

If you decide that attitudes are critical to follow-through in your company, what are the right attitudes?

The Right *Attitudes?*

AOL would have never become such a success story in its early days had they not learned to hire for attitudes over experience.

In 1997, AOL had just passed the ten-million-subscribers mark. A new source of revenues, representing billions in additional profits, literally showed up at the company's front door. The chief executive of a feisty new long-distance carrier, Tele-Save, arrived with a check for $50 million. He wanted AOL to sell him the first big Internet sponsorship (or portal) deal.

Interest from other companies followed quickly—start-ups and established players alike began nosing around for marketing partnerships and banner ads. AOL's execs realized they needed many more advertising account managers and (what AOL dubbed) business affairs specialists to manage this lucrative new business.

So the senior VPs of Interactive Marketing ran ads and contacted recruiters. "We're looking for people who are Internet savvy but also have ten years of marketing or sales experience in a field like consumer products or automotive," their ads ran. And indeed, frontline managers and HR screened and hired people with ten years of the appropriate experience.

Unhappily, many of those new hires ended up not being very good at promoting or selling portal deals. So a couple of maverick HR people from AOL's Office of Organizational Effectiveness took a step back. They studied the company's best dealmakers, comparing the skills they had and the skills of the poorer performers.

When they analyzed their findings, they realized that experience wasn't what separated the best dealmakers at AOL from the so-so performers. In fact, they were surprised to learn that often ten years of experience was an accurate predictor of *poor* performance. AOL's top people in ad sales and marketing shared five characteristics that had nothing to do with their years spent in marketing:

- **Learning agility.** The top performers were people who caught on quickly and were able to switch direction at a moment's notice.
- **Able to deal with ambiguity.** A lack of anxiety in high-pressure, fast-changing situations was another trait shared by the best. AOL's top dealmakers could confidently make decisions without having all the data, and without obsessing over uncertainty.
- **Influence over others (especially in presentations).** AOL's best salespeople had a lot of ego drive—an overwhelming desire to

convince, to get agreement, and close the deal. They were also great on their feet, able to phrase their ideas convincingly and quickly.

- **Able to work without supervision.** AOL's was a fast-and-loose culture. Those who were self-motivated and able to do well without intense supervision outperformed those who needed more supervision.

- **Good networking skills.** It took a lot of cooperation to get things done at AOL. Sales and marketing people needed to get what they required from other departments that didn't answer to the same bosses. That required strong social skills (like the ability to win the support of others) as well as an ability to persevere after being told no many times.

Taking that list of five behaviors, Michael Drake, then an executive in AOL's Office of Organizational Effectiveness and Corporate Staffing Group, began helping the VPs and front-line managers search for these traits as they screened new applicants. He built profiles of the ideal candidate for the position, and created questions to help uncover candidates' attitudes.

The results were fantastic. AOL's portal deals quickly grew into a billion-dollar business. In the first three months of 2000, AOL's new dealmakers had booked an amazing $721 million in sales and created a $2.4-billion backlog. (The "sky's the limit" projections for portal revenues were one of the primary reasons AOL was such a hot stock and able to attract Time Warner into one of the world's biggest media mergers.)

"These new people are the best people we've ever hired," one of the VPs told Drake. "They've even helped us realize that the people we thought were stars really aren't!"

AOL took the time to identify the personality qualities that were important for the job, profile their people, segregate the best from the rest, and then analyze the traits of the top performers. Then they used those new criteria to screen new applicants to find people with the attitudes that would best succeed in their organization.

Any manager in a big or small company can use that same general formula. All it takes is a willingness to put aside one's assumptions about the importance of experience, and a desire to uncover the traits that are important in your own business or department.

Dr. Sarah Bridges is an executive coach and doctor of psychology who specializes in organizational effectiveness. In her practice she assesses jobs and people to assure a good fit between the two. And Bridges completely agrees with John's (from the taxpayer support line) and Drake's conclusions. "I am not one for hiring experience," she said emphatically.

"Reading résumés and the rest seldom works out. When hiring, it is critical to differentiate between the things that can be learned and things that are highly resistant to change," Bridges explained. "By the time we are twenty-five years old, our personalities are largely set. Attitudes and interpersonal style are much harder to modify [than technical skills and industry-specific know-how]."

For that reason, Bridges feels managers need to become more educated about people and their personal chemistry. Bridges calls this "learning to be more psychologically minded." Becoming psychologically minded means learning a framework for understanding people's personalities and connecting that framework to the behavior that best fits your business goals.

A Framework for Personality

Psychologists have studied the human personality in order to predict behavior for a century. Many different models have been proposed. In the last decade, one particular model gained broad acceptance. It is called the "Big Five."

The "Big Five" traits of human personality are:

1. Conscientiousness

Conscientiousness is a person's inclination to be responsible, careful, well-organized, persevering, and diligent. People who show a lack of conscientiousness are easily distracted or exhibit inconsistent, impulsive, unreliable, or irresponsible behavior. Conscientious people sweat the small stuff (which in the extreme turns into obsessive questioning and demands for clarifications). High scorers are methodical, driven to exceed expectations, and dutiful. However, highly conscientious people can also be less spontaneous and less charming than those who are less conscientious.

2. Openness

Openness is the degree to which an individual is broad-minded, curious, insightful, and original. Highly conservative, imitative, and overly cautious behavior shows a lack of openness. High scorers tend to be imaginative, creative, seeking out cultural and educational experiences. They are unable to understand the dictum "if it ain't broke, don't fix it." They seek out change. Low scorers are more down-to-earth, realistic, less interested in what's new, tend to repeat past behavior, and are more comfortable with routine tasks.

3. Agreeableness

Agreeableness is personified in someone who is forgiving, kind, courteous, and supportive. Skeptical, guarded, self-centered, hardheaded, or indifferent behavior is the polar opposite of agreeableness. People high in agreeableness tend to be trusting, humble, and cooperative. Low scorers tend to be more aggressive, less sympathetic, and less team-oriented.

4. Extroversion

Psychological pioneer Carl Jung originated the term *extrovert* to explain a disposition that was outgoing, gregarious, sociable, talkative, ambitious, and thrill-seeking. Quiet people—people who are shy, introspective, reserved, or aloof—are often more introverted. Extroversion is linked to assertiveness or ego drive, the desire to convince and to be convincing. Introversion is linked to more solitary interests, reflection, and deeper analysis.

5. Emotional Stability

Emotionally stable people are measured, appropriate, calm, secure, rational, and optimistic. People with less emotional stability are anxious, angry, insecure, defensive, tense, and often sad. Low scorers are prone to impulsiveness, and can be easily discouraged. They are more likely to blame external forces for setbacks. High scorers tend to be more relaxed, tolerant, able to work under pressure, and able to handle frustration.

Connecting the Big Five to Your Hiring

According to Bridges, a good fit between a job candidate and the organization depends on many variables—the manager's goals, the company culture, the customers, the team, your boss, and YOU. Managers need to make an accurate assessment of the real conditions in their work before they decide what kind of person is likely to thrive in those conditions.

Ask yourself:

What behaviors are required? How much problem-solving, autonomy, learning ability, interpersonal skills, etc., do I need?

What kinds of people tend to fail? What kinds of people make it? (Use the Big Five to score each.)

How do I rate myself using the Big Five? How do others rate me? How do I rate my boss? How do I rate the corporate culture? Does your company prize extroverted people? Agreeable associates? Does the company have problems with creative types (high scorers on openness) or people who need a lot of hand-holding (low scorers on emotional stability)?

For example: How important is conscientiousness? If you look again at the list of traits AOL looked for, conscientiousness is not important among their top performers. There's a good reason for that. AOL wanted to capitalize on the interest potential clients had in a portal deals fast—too fast for AOL's people to develop a thorough understanding of what really worked and what was a waste of a client's money. This is typical in advertising sales. If you are managing a team that believes the old adage "you can't make an omelet without breaking some eggs," you don't want people who are so highly conscientious that they will hesitate closing the deal. (One can argue that overlooking the value of conscientiousness and emotional stability led to AOL's subsequent troubles, as we'll see later.)

Now go back to the questions at the beginning of this chapter. How important are problem solving, autonomy, adaptability, being good with people, maturity, ego drive, and decisiveness to your execution and follow-through? Try linking those behaviors with the Big Five personality traits. Now you're ready to rough out a profile of the traits and behaviors you need to screen for.

For example:

TRAITS I NEED
(rank the top need as six and the bottom need as one)

Solution skills (problem solving)—the capacity to see a variety of win-win approaches to challenges, to overcome limitations and use creativity.

1	2	3	4	5	6

Likely traits: openness, emotional stability, and conscientiousness.

Empathy (good with people)—the ability to *anticipate* the feelings, thoughts, and actions of another, and to use that understanding to help or lead others.

1	2	3	4	5	6

Likely traits: a higher level of agreeableness, openness, and emotional stability.

Commitment (maturity)—the willingness to deal with unpleasant or demanding responsibilities, to live up to others' expectations, and to go outside one's comfort zone.

1	2	3	4	5	6

Likely traits: conscientiousness and emotional stability.

Assertiveness (ego drive)—the ability to hold one's own in competitive situations, to handle deadlines, and do good when put on the spot.

1	2	3	4	5	6

Likely traits: extroversion; watch out for too much agreeableness.

Flexibility (adaptability)—enough self-worth to consider change, the ability to see the big picture and be pragmatic.

1   2   3   4   5   6

Likely traits: emotional stability and openness.

Self-drive (autonomy)—the ability to accomplish things without supervision, to work well, and to use personal discretion to juggle priorities.

1   2   3   4   5   6

Likely traits: extroversion and conscientiousness.

NOTES ON USING THE BIG FIVE FRAMEWORK

Experts have created an almost endless list of terms and phrases to describe the components of human personality. Each expert has devotees and detractors. So if you're a proponent of the Myers-Briggs personality test (or a user of some other branded service), please don't conclude that the Big Five is the only way to become more psychologically minded. I use the Big Five simply because it is one of the most widely respected tools for dissecting personalities into traits *and* is easy for most managers to link with business behavior.

But whether you use the Big Five or any other framework to gain understanding, remember the following guidelines:

- **Don't go to extremes.** Rather than labeling people as one thing or another, you should always think of each trait as part of a continuum. Every trait exists in all of us to various degrees. If you rate most people on a scale (from one to seven, for example), you'll find they tend to fall someplace in the middle, rather than at either end.

- **Don't think in black and white.** There are both positive and negative aspects to any trait. For example, highly conscientiousness people may not be spontaneous, highly imaginative people can get bored quickly, self-sufficient candidates often aren't good in team settings, and many warm and agreeable personalities have trouble being tough when toughness is called for. Even emotional stability has its negative side. A lot of drive has its roots in insecurity; productive urgency can be a by-product of unproductive anger. Don't forget the yin and yang of every aspect of one's personality. Try not to think in simple black-and-white terms.

- **Remember, you're trying to become more psychologically minded, not a psychologist.** "A manager doesn't need to be a psychologist any more than a lifeguard needs to be a doctor," says organizational psychologist Dr. Harry Levinson. Don't use the Big Five or Myers-Briggs assessments (or any other system) to analyze everyone around you. If you need a professional psychological analysis, hire an expert. The purpose of this chapter is to make you a more knowledgeable observer so you can assist others and become a better decision-maker.

- **Expect ambiguity.** Analyzing traits to predict behavior is something any manager can do, but they must have the temperament to deal with some ambiguity.

  Understanding how to link traits to behavior is a soft science without hard answers. The only way to find out what traits your team members need is to educate yourself, use your knowledge and gut instincts to make decisions, make mistakes, and learn from them.

  Hiring based on attitudes is something new. And as Harvard's Theodore Levitt famously advised, *the only way to deal with what's new is by being widely informed and thinking straight . . . there are no easy formulas or exotic textbook models to rely on.*

- **Make sure you are thinking straight.** Follow the guidelines in "More Accurate Assessments": Put your thoughts on paper, look below the surface, open yourself up, and get feedback on your conclusions from your friends, family, boss, colleagues, and subordinates. Find a group of like-minded individuals to discuss psychological issues. Feedback is very important, according to Dr. Bridges. "Many managers get almost no accurate feedback," she said. "That's how leaders end up with tremendous Achilles' heels."

- **Invest the time.** Bridges knows that becoming more psychologically minded takes time. But it's worth it. "Technically sound managers are a dime a dozen. The person who develops an aptitude for understanding different people and being versatile is unique. This is going to be the differentiating factor in the most successful managers," according to Bridges.

HOW TO SCREEN FOR THE RIGHT ATTITUDES

Businesses often fail to grow because they don't know how to select the right people for their teams.

Managers fail to find the right fit because they don't develop the skills to conduct a top-notch screening interview, often expecting some mental checklist to give them enough insight. "Competent interviewers can elicit a much more complete [and useful] picture of a candidate than any [personality] inventory can," writes Dr. Harry Levinson.*

Here are some tips for screening interviews that will help you uncover a candidate's personality traits based on past behavior.

- **Plan your interview in advance.** Too many managers try to wing it, or take a few minutes to think about an hourlong interview. *Prepare.* Read over the application or résumé; look for experiences that, when discussed, will reveal a candidate's personality traits. For example, if you're trying to gauge their learning agility, Dr. Bridges suggests that you find a point in their work history where they got in over their head, took on a big project, or entered an unfamiliar environment. "Ask, 'What went as you expected? What took you by surprise? What mistakes did you make? What did you learn?'" Dr. Bridges advises. "Some people have no thoughts, some give only empty answers. The person who has a high desire to learn will launch right into it and say, 'This is what I learned and this is how I applied it.'" Make a list of what you're looking for and what questions might help you discern the behavior you are looking for.
- **Get them talking freely.** Many interviewers do far too much talking to learn what they need to know about the applicant.

---

*Dr. Harry Levinson, "Pitfalls of Personality Tests," *The Levinson Letter*, 1992.

That's partly because the manager is not prepared. But it's also because managers don't know how to get people to talk freely. You want your candidate to forget this is a job interview and talk without restriction. The easiest way is to ask, "Tell me about yourself." Nine times out of ten, the interviewee will reply, "Where should I begin?" Tell them, "Begin with 'I was born in [place, not date] . . .' and we'll go from there." That breaks the ice quickly and lets you begin to steer into a discussion of their background and early significant experiences. Don't be overly businesslike. Converse as if you were chatting with a colleague. Use your natural curiosity. When you come across something that sounds important, ask, "What did you learn?" and "Do you regret missing any experiences? Have you thought about what you'd like to understand better or skills you'd like to have?" Develop your ability to get people to talk freely.

- **Ask about what they did, not what they think.** When discussing their experiences at work, ask about specific examples in real situations rather than hypotheticals. Instead of asking, "How would you handle an irate customer?" say, "Give me an example of a time where you had to confront an angry customer." Their story will provide clues to their abilities—how they handled aggression, how they see themselves as a problem solver, what lengths they will go to get the job done, or how creative, agreeable, and fair they are.

    Some other good revealing questions tied to what they did are:
    1. What made your favorite boss so good? Tell me about a time she did something you admired.
    2. What things tend to push your buttons? Give me an example of a time when someone pushed them.
    3. What helps you do your best work? Tell me about a time when that happened.

- **Don't get fooled.** We've all been fooled. The interviewee starts telling you what you want to hear or answering questions to project an image that's not genuine. In psychological testing they call that a "fake good." To avoid fake goods in live interviews, your best bet is to:

Trust your gut. Turn your radar on high, just as you would if you were meeting your son/daughter's date or college roommates. If you feel something's not right, it might be your subconscious giving you valid feedback. Ask more questions. Don't make excuses or be shy. You should expect to be seeing somebody at their best. Any negative feelings are too important to gloss over.

Get a second opinion. Some women have better and quicker "people radar" than men. If you are a man, arrange for the candidate to wait an extra five minutes; have a female associate of yours chat with them. Get her first impressions after the candidate leaves. Or have another manager sit in on your interview, and later get that manager's impressions. It's important to stress to your "second opinion" that you are looking for gut-level reactions, not an intricate analysis.

Take your time and then some. A wise old entrepreneur advised, "Just about everybody can say the right things for thirty minutes. Exhaust their thirty minutes of charm and then ask all your questions again." For that reason especially, it's a good practice to do at least three interviews with qualified candidates for key positions, with two of them lasting at least an hour. Following each interview, make notes on what you've learned, what you want to learn the next time, and what you need to confirm.

One executive I know conducted three interviews with a candidate and still wasn't completely comfortable. She wasn't sure if it was her or him. Near the conclusion of the third interview, the manager asked, "What additional information do you want from me?" The candidate immediately replied, "How many more interviews?" with a hint of exasperation. The executive, a very quick study, instantly shot back, "Three!" That was all it took for him to break. "I don't have the time or patience for that," he told her as he left. "Cool," she thought, "I just saved myself from a real headache."

See how they deal with conflict. It's possible to be too nice in an interview. One manager said, "I'll heckle my candidate. I'll purposely disagree with something they said just to see how they handle conflict." That's a good idea. It can reveal someone's character and help you answer some important questions: Can the candidate stay charming while defending their point of view? Do they give in to pressure too fast? Do they ask questions to understand the conflict before continuing to argue? You can learn a lot from creating some tension in an interview and not being so nice.

Keep assessing after you hire. Managers stop their attitudes assessment too soon. Most states give you a ninety-day probationary period where you can change your mind. You should use that to your advantage, according to Dr. Bridges. It's easy, she says, to make excuses for a new hire in the first ninety days, convincing yourself:

- It takes a while to get comfortable.
- He came to us from a very different work culture.
- The work isn't easy and I haven't given her enough time to get acclimated.
- I don't like to make snap judgments.

According to Dr. Bridges, "During the first ninety days of a job, [new hires] are in the romantic, *put your best foot forward* period of dating." Dr. Bridges advises, "If the person isn't behaving during those first ninety days, I wouldn't have high hopes for the marriage."

It is obvious when someone is not hitting the mark. If you have even the slightest question, *take off your rose-colored glasses* and say, "Hey, no excuses." Very few organizations are on the ball enough to do an accurate assessment within the first ninety days, but it's critically important to having the right people for your goals.

Use the "iceberg" analogy: Whatever you see in the first three months is just the tip of the iceberg—there is much more below the surface. Test any negative signals a new hire sends during that period. Be sure you are satisfied with her before she becomes a permanent fixture.

POSTSCRIPT

Everybody now knows the sad saga of AOL. Against all odds, they rose to become the biggest success story of the Internet economy and to merge with one of the world's greatest content companies. Then, in 2003, AOL lost its luster, and in 2004 the name AOL Time Warner was shortened back to just Time Warner. One reason for the radical reassessment was the stunning slide in revenues from AOL's portal deals.

From a high of $721 million in online advertising in the first quarter of 2000, AOL's revenue fell 69 percent in just three years.

Andy Kessler, in his *Wall Street Journal* article "The Sinking Case of AOL Time Warner," concluded, "It [AOL] was a house of cards . . . hooked on advertising [revenues]." And when those revenues stalled, the bosses panicked.

There are many reasons for AOL's dramatic fall from grace, but one is especially important to managers who are hiring for attitude. As Michael Drake explains:

> We neglected to look at the downside of bringing in exclusively type A people with those proven dealmaker traits. They had the skills to talk people into anything, and they did. Sometimes their attention to detail was so poor. One *forgot* how many impressions we could deliver in an hour and promised [a big customer] four times what our system was capable of delivering!

And when clients called to complain about being overpromised and underdelivered, according to Drake, those same people were heard arrogantly cursing at the clients. AOL hadn't balanced their teams with personal qualities other than type A traits, extroversion and openness (and, to a lesser degree, agreeableness). They were low on both conscientiousness, the trait that would have prevented overpromising and underdelivering, and emotional stability, which would have countered the impulse to berate clients.

AOL made a perfectly understandable mistake. The company

had measured their top dealmakers at a time when portal deals were brand new and their business was on a tremendous growth curve. The top performers were great at *finding* customers, but they didn't have the conscientiousness and emotional stability for *keeping* customers and growing them. The latter wasn't AOL's primary focus during those years. Retaining customers became important only when the company's growth stalled.

The bigger mistake was that AOL's top brass didn't listen to their front-line managers who saw that many megaclients weren't satisfied with the portal deals and AOL's attitude. And when it became obvious that clients were defecting, AOL didn't reexamine their hiring criteria.

Who knows? Perhaps if they had reassessed their hiring criteria, that famous acronym "AOL" might still be in the Time Warner name. Clearly, those bosses didn't have the right attitudes for fast-changing times.

5 MATCH EVERYONE'S AGENDA

■

For more than forty years, managers have been told that if they follow the simple formula of do *"this"* and you'll get *"that,"* their people will follow through consistently.

It's the world's most popular prescription for motivating and directing workers, theoretically supported by science. Behaviorist B. F. Skinner showed that groups of pigeons and rats could be conditioned to ring a bell each time they wanted food. Skinner believed that human behavior was like that of lab animals, leading managers to assume that people will follow through better when they are conditioned to expect some sort of a targeted reward.

Today, three out of four big organizations use stock options, commissions, bonuses, trips to exotic locales, and the like in the place of Skinner's food pellets to make sure what's expected gets done.

When executives at these organizations are confronted with the fact that half (or more) of what they expected to get done has fallen through the cracks, most assume it's because they failed to reward the right things. They fine-tune the mix between their targets, incentives, and consequences. If that first fine-tuning doesn't cure the situation, managers simply go back and tinker with the mix yet again.

But one newly promoted executive (let's call her Nancy) stepped back from this endless loop of failure and tinkering with incentives to take a path less traveled. When her plan for a business turnaround stalled, she stopped to ask herself why. As she peeled away the layers of her team's failure to follow through, she discovered what social scientist Alfie Kohn had been trying to get across to management for years. "No controlled scientific study has ever found a long-term enhancement of the quality of work as a result of any reward system,"* he argued. At best, they offer a short-term fix. "They do not create an enduring commitment to any value or action."† In other words, *do this and you'll get that* won't help encourage people to follow through.

"My own follow-through wasn't really motivated by my bonus," Nancy realized. Instead, it was the connection that she felt between her personal goals, her professional goals, and the goals of the business unit that compelled her commitment.

That discovery led to an "a-ha" moment. If everyone on Nancy's team felt a similar match between their personal goals and the goals of the division, she reasoned, maybe they'd have the same motivation to follow through.

Matching everyone's agendas worked for that enterprising manager. In just one year, Nancy's division went from being a chronic underperformer to consistently hitting their turnaround goals.

This section explains what you can do to match your team's agendas to your business plan, explaining how to get your people's personal goals and professional objectives in line.

THE "A-HA" MOMENT

"In our president's mind, I was taking over a lost cause," recalled Nancy, a newly promoted vice president. "My division's revenues

*Alfie Kohn, "Challenging Behaviorist Dogma: Myths About Money and Motivation," *Compensation and Benefits Review*, March/April 1998.
†Alfie Kohn, "Why Incentive Plans Cannot Work," *Harvard Business Review*, Vol. 71, Issue 5, Sept./Oct. 1993.

and margins had declined for three straight years and all our competitors were experiencing problems in that same product category. Our top executives thought I should figure out how to downsize the company's financial exposure over the next year and start reducing everyone's expectations."

But this was Nancy's first big, vice-president-level assignment, and she was eager to show her bosses she could do more than just hold the line on a faltering business unit—she could turn it around.

So the new VP dug in. She completed a comprehensive examination of the opportunities and challenges in her category and uncovered several strong possibilities for improvement. Next she generated some fresh ideas to take advantage of those opportunities. Then she convinced her immediate supervisor to free up a few resources. Last, Nancy communicated her plan to revive the division to her entire team, rolled up her sleeves, and started following through.

But after six months of effort, nothing much had changed.

"Why?" she asked herself. "It's not that I was too optimistic," she thought. "The potential is there and the plan is right. My people just aren't motivated enough to follow through. I don't get it."

So she asked herself why four more times:

Why aren't my people motivated?

"Our bonuses depend on turning this division around," she thought. "None of us will get a better opportunity if we don't make this thing work first. So everyone's got the right incentives and consequences [the *do this and you'll get that* formula]. They're just not as committed as I am."

Why not?

Nancy reflected on what made her so enthused. It wasn't the bonus. While Nancy did have a significant incentive program, her total compensation would be the same (and probably easier to achieve) if she simply reduced the financial exposure and everyone's expectations. Her more aggressive turnaround goal actually made achieving her bonus *less likely*.

Instead, she realized it was intangibles other than the bonus that motivated her.

- *It was her big chance to impress the people who promoted her.* In other words, a successful turnaround would improve her chances of getting to the next level.

- *It was her opportunity to prove to herself that she had what it takes.* It was her chance to prove to herself she knew what she was doing and had the skills to succeed despite challenging business conditions.

- *It was her chance to feel like a real leader.* Her team had missed their budgets (and therefore their bonuses and any chances to be promoted) for two straight years. Nancy imagined how good it would feel to be seen as the one who made everyone's life better by helping them to earn more money and opportunities—part of her definition of a real leader.

Nancy had somehow connected the dots between her personal goals, her professional goal, and a clear understanding of the investment in time and effort *she* was willing to make to turn around the division. It was this complete connection that made Nancy feel so committed.

Why haven't my associates made their own connection?

Nancy's agenda match had occurred naturally, without any coaching by her bosses. Her associate's agendas weren't as well matched because that match hadn't occurred to them naturally. And she hadn't done anything to help them along.

Why don't I help create the same match for each member of my team?

So she went back to her team and asked each person about their history, challenges, and dreams—and got them to tell her their own expectations for their professional and personal lives. Next she analyzed their strengths, and the gaps between their current abilities and what would be required for them to meet their personal goals. Then Nancy compared what she learned about each person's individual agenda with what she believed she needed for a successful turnaround. As a result, she recast her people and plans, focusing everyone on the connection between the business objectives, each individual's plan, and the team's vision of a better future for everyone.

Within six months, she had matched 75 percent of her people to the turnaround plan. Six months after that, everybody was on the same page.

Follow-through in her division soared. Her team cleaned up the mess that accumulated in their unit during the down years and began hitting their highly ambitious turnaround targets. This commitment endured, and for the first time in years the unit achieved its yearly budget.

"Originally, I thought it would be *my plan* that would turn this business unit around," she explained. "But it wasn't. It was the people. As I aligned with their goals, they aligned with mine. Once we all saw the connection between their hopes for the future and the plan to turn the division around, I got the follow-through I needed."

WHY MATCHING EVERYONE'S AGENDA WORKED

Back in the fifties, Fred Herzberg, author of *The Motivation to Work*, challenged conventional wisdom when he discovered that what makes people happy about their work and what makes them unhappy about their work were different things. What makes them happy, he wrote, are achievement, recognition, autonomy, challenge, and growth. What makes them unhappy includes working conditions, security, their relationships with peers and bosses, company policies, quality of supervision, and *compensation*. Herzberg's research suggested that a good compensation program, at best, eliminates dissatisfaction. But it doesn't motivate.

Since 1959, academics (and compensation consultants) have taken issue with Herzberg's conclusions, arguing that earnings can be much more than a cause of workplace dissatisfaction. Pay also can significantly affect worker satisfaction, they claim, arguing that how much one makes affects one's feelings about achievement, autonomy, and growth. They also point out that to squeeze out the inequities and emotions that can make the workplace unfair (and make associates unhappy), managers need some kind of rational rewards system. Pay for performance, they claim, is the most rational incentive.

But arguing such fine points about compensation's role as a motivator misses Herzberg's more important insight. What gets people excited and what causes them to be apathetic, he discovered, *are many different things*. Each individual defines satisfaction and dissatisfaction in their own way—and prioritizes what makes them happy differently. Their perceptions depend on their personality, their personal situation, the working conditions, and the job they are expected to do. As a result, managers have no alternative but to understand each associate's expectations (and their willingness to accept trade-offs) in order to match the right people to the plan and goals of a business unit.

Matching agendas does not require a manager to reject or endorse the idea of using financial incentives to reward their people. Matching agendas simply recognizes that a one-size-fits-all scramble for financial rewards won't necessarily make your people happy.

Unless a manager understands each associate's agenda, and matches each individual's goals to their unit's goals, he or she will fall short of getting an enduring commitment to follow through.

That's what Nancy learned as she fixed her own follow-through process. Matching everyone's agenda gave her an accurate assessment of the fit between each team member and her goals for the division. Integrating her team's expectations into her planning and using their motivation to inspire and direct follow-through made all the difference.

MATCHING AGENDAS

Once you understand the basics of creating a clear direction, matching everyone's agenda to it can be as easy as one, two, three.

One, start by getting each of your team member's individual expectations.

Two, follow that with a reality check—your accurate assessment of what it will take to achieve their expectations and your team's perceptions of the investment they are willing to make to meet their targets.

Three, put the pieces together—fit what you've learned about each associate's expectations to the goals of the business unit. Some people may need to be reassigned. Goals may need to be adjusted.

As one manager who succeeded with this process said, "Whatever it took, we gave it to them and it worked."

Step One: Get Each Team Member's Individual Expectations

The only way you'll ever discover your team members' expectations is by asking them.

You'll learn a lot from such a dialogue. Some people will tell you they expect to achieve a great deal with little investment of time or other resources. Others will be too guarded to answer thoroughly and honestly, showing that they don't trust you. Still others will claim you are the first manager to ever show such an interest and then tell all without any prodding. Whatever their response, it will be an eye-opening experience. When it's over, you'll wonder why you haven't been asking your people to share their expectations with you your entire career.

Before taking this first step, go back and review the principles of negotiating your boss's expectations in the chapters titled "Clear Expectations" and "Read Between the Lines."

- Take another look at the dos and don'ts of listening.
- Review the section on gaining trust.
- Turn your gut-level radar on high so you can read between the lines.

Then schedule a session with everyone on your team. Be up front, and explain the purpose of the meeting. For example, "I'm sure you've noticed I'm paying a lot more attention to getting clear expectations from headquarters on what's expected of us. I was thinking the other day I should do the same with you, so I clearly understand just what you expect from me. I'd like to sit down and spend some time getting your views on what success looks like for you over the next year or two."

Start the conversation as you would with a job applicant. Review their personal and job history. Establish a rapport with each team member, using the tools you've learned to confirm trust. If you can't get them comfortable, find out why and fix the problem. (And if there is no way you can get them to trust you and open up, doesn't that tell you everything you need to know about their ability to fit into your plans?)

Once you've got a good rapport going, it's time to learn what their specific expectations are. Here are some questions you might use:

- *What would you like to be earning in the next twelve months? In twenty-four months? In five years?*

    Why? What would you do with that money? (Their personal priorities)

    What kind of percentage income increase would that take? (Some perspective on the practicality of their expectations)

    Have you ever accomplished a similar increase in earnings? (A reality check)

    Tell me what you did to get that increase? (More reality)

- *What professional advancement would you like to achieve in the next two years and in five years?*

    Have you been promoted like that in the past?

    Tell me what you did to earn that kind of advancement?

    What new skills did you master?

    What accomplishments preceded the promotion?

- *What do you believe are your top three skills that qualify you for this job?* (Ask for examples that prove these are skills that they possess and make a difference in their work.)

- *What would you like to be able to do better? What else?* (Asking what else is an easy way to get below the surface. Continue to ask "what else" nicely until they can't think of anything else.)

- *What do you need from me?*

By asking these kinds of questions, one executive at a technology company discovered his people expected double and triple the earnings they were likely to make. "They were told by the executives that hired them to expect to make over a million dollars a year," he explained. "But nobody told them this million-dollar compensation program assumed a huge increase in the value of their future stock options—which in the year 2000 looked very unlikely."

It was no wonder his people weren't following through, he decided. They felt the company didn't follow through on their promises about pay (which, as Herzberg concluded, is a major source of dissatisfaction).

As he continued to talk to his people, that executive learned that many had earned big paychecks in previous jobs, but those jobs lacked opportunities for personal growth or had difficult working conditions. Several people explained they would gladly "trade off" some of their income expectations for a better environment and chances to be promoted (as Herzberg predicted).

Since it was unlikely that the stock options would continue to make every employee an instant millionaire, those trade-offs became a critical part of his plan for matching everyone's individual agenda to the unit's plan.

Step Two: The Reality Check

Once you get each associate's personal and professional expectations out on the table, follow up with what they are willing to invest.

Many associates don't realize that they must invest more time, money, or effort to get further in their career. They believe that greater rewards come simply through putting in your time and gaining tenure. These days that's a fatal mistake. If an associate expects to create a different (and better) future, they need to make an investment in learning new skills, becoming more productive, or taking on more responsibility before they are promoted. Prepare them to do their part by getting each associate to think about what it is worth to them to reach their goals in real tangible terms.

Ask them:

- *What kind of time, money, and effort would you invest to reach these goals?*

    Would you invest hours beyond the normal workweek to reach your goals? Tell me about a time when you made that kind of investment.

    If the plan to achieve your goals required a personal financial investment, could you make it? Tell me about a time when you spent a significant amount of money gaining new skills, or on technology tools that helped your career.

> *Have you ever persevered on something difficult and suc-*
> *ceeded? Tell me about it....*

Finding out what advancement is worth to each team member is critical. If what he or she is willing to invest is not sufficient, the manager must either negotiate the associate's expectations down or his or her investment up. And if there is no way to make this a sensible match, you're better off knowing that now.

ANOTHER WAY TO EXPLORE WHAT A TEAM MEMBER WILL INVEST TO REACH HIS OR HER GOALS

Some managers are uncomfortable with direct questions about personal goals and investment. And some employees are reluctant to give extra effort when doing so in the past has gotten them little in return.

Another way to get your people to tell you what they're willing to do to reach their goals is to close your review of those goals with an assignment. Say something like this:

> I'm going to take what you've told me and think about what I can do to help you reach these goals. While I'm working on that, I'd like you to take forty-eight hours to prepare an answer to one last question.
>
> Imagine it's now the end of our year. We're on track for hitting your goals. I have just given you a great review, complimenting your work and grading your contribution to the team goals as "exceeding my expectations." In a paragraph or two, please tell me, as you look back at this great year, what you did to earn this glowing review.

This is an easy exercise to get associates to focus on the extra effort and investment they need to make to achieve their goals.

And this assignment creates a tangible commitment that the manager can use during the year for reenergizing follow-through.

TROUBLESHOOTING YOUR AGENDA

The day was like every other that week, starting very early and ending very late. A management consultant, Ray, was sitting in a restaurant in South Florida with his friend and client, Robert. They were having a casual conversation when Robert asked Ray a pointed question. "What do you believe is holding you back?" he said. "I'm sure you're constantly analyzing where you are against where you'd like to be," Robert explained, "and thinking about what obstacles are in your way." He grabbed a cocktail napkin and suggested, "Let's make a list."

Robert was right. Ray had spent many nights thinking about where he'd like to be. And it always led to thoughts of all the disadvantages he faced—a bad economy, customers who didn't believe in spending money training their people, associates who weren't as committed as he was . . . all the things he'd wished were different so he could hit his goals.

"Well," Ray began, "a new business always has a tough time establishing credibility."

"Okay," Robert said, and jotted a note: "credibility is number one."

Ray quickly added, "A lot of the things that would get me ahead are outside my budget."

"Money is number two," Robert said, and wrote that down.

They went on like that for a couple of napkins. Then Robert stopped Ray. "I'm looking over this list and it's very comprehensive," Robert said. "You've obviously given this question a lot of thought. But you know, I see one thing is missing from your list."

He paused, and then, looking Ray right in the eye, he said, "Ray . . . you're not on it."

No matter how good your plan is, it's going to run into some obstacles. But just how formidable those obstacles are depends on your perspective. If you put your head to the floor and look up at a hindrance, it can appear insurmountable. On the other hand, from another angle many problems look like molehills. In other words, the way *you* look at a problem may be part of the problem.

It's important to adjust your employees' perspective when matching everyone's agenda. People need to understand that roadblocks are inevitable and are something they must overcome. They have to take personal responsibility for their success.

Try the exercise Robert used with Ray. Ask your employee for a list, a review of the bureaucratic hurdles, the limited resources, the unexpected challenges, and the like that have kept him or her from hitting goals. Take the list seriously; talk about what you can do to help smooth the path. But also see if they put themselves on that list. If not, tell them about Ray and Robert.

It's a great way to get someone to realize that they, too, are responsible.

Step Three: Piece the Puzzle Together

When you give a team member who's willing to make a sizable investment of time and perseverance a blank sheet of paper and clear expectations, he or she will likely get very creative. Planning how to hit everyone's goals and following through once the agendas are matched up is the fun part.

And what do you do with those people who don't make a match? You don't necessarily have to fire them, although you may help some to transfer to another business unit where they can better thrive. Remember, the fact that your agendas don't match isn't a crime. But having someone on your team who's not in a position to succeed is a real transgression. This process will encourage difficult, inflexible, or other poorly matched associates to look for another opportunity. Your responsibility is making that happen on *your* schedule.

When you think about it, it makes perfect sense that people would be more inspired and motivated when they see the connection between their own goals and what the business unit expects to accomplish.

It's equally obvious that if the sum total of each individual's goals don't match a business unit's goals, success is unlikely.

But matching agendas are not obvious.

- Forty-eight percent of employees and managers have no clear idea of the link between their daily efforts and the company's goals.
- Forty-seven percent of employees believe their bonus program isn't fair or sensible.
- Fifty-one percent can't see the value of their performance-review program to the company.

To overcome such a disconnect, get your people to tell you what they expect, make sure that fits with your own expectations, and then put the pieces together.

6 FIND A CHAMPION

W hen the head of marketing for Canadian Pacific Hotels
was asked to increase his company's revenues from business travelers, he knew he couldn't just copy some giant hotel
chain's loyalty program. Research showed that these "rewards"
schemes—offering business guests points similar to airline miles
for every dollar spent—were too expensive to administer for
smaller companies like CP Hotels (now the Fairmont Hotels and
Resorts). In fact, when McKinsey consultants analyzed many
rewards programs, they concluded that a majority failed to give
companies a good return on investment.*

"Business clients are the most demanding and discerning customers in the hospitality industry," marketing chief Brian Richardson says. So he asked these travelers what, besides points, would get
them to come back again and again. After talking to scores of travelers, he found that beyond bonus points they all wanted a more
personalized experience, one where each stay was based on their
individual likes and dislikes.

---

*J. Cigliano, M. Georgiadis, D. Pleasance, and S. Whalley, "The Price of Loyalty," *The
McKinsey Quarterly*, No. 4, 2000.

So Richardson's team sat down and mapped out all the possibilities, from choices in room location to having their favorite soft drink in the minibar, and every other moment of the guest experience, from checking in to checking out. For each point of contact (and there were dozens) and every option, Richardson's team prescribed new, higher service standards, inventing what they called a "President's Club" level of hospitality for Fairmont's business clientele.

The promise to prospective Fairmont President's Club (FPC) members was simple—you tell us what you want and we'll move heaven and earth to get it for you every time you stay with us, anywhere in the world.

"Easy to say," Richardson's associate Jon Mamela explained. "But we knew following through was going to be very difficult."

Mamela was brought in to lead this new initiative in relationship marketing. He and his team put together a training program, a detailed list of specific procedures, numerous checklists, and job descriptions. They created a sophisticated database and information-distribution system so that every hotel would receive all the direction they needed for personalizing each FPC member's stay on a daily basis.

"But there's so much that needs to get done day in and day out—what we call *setting up the house*—necessary to make this program work," Mamela said. "We were afraid that if we just added this [the special requirements for each President's Club member] to the general manager's to-do list, something important could end up falling through the cracks."

Instead of mandating this new initiative and leaving the follow-through to the existing managers, the executive team decided to create the position of FPC Champion in every hotel. "The champion is the central hub, making certain the house is set up correctly for all incoming members [which can be almost half of all non-group reservations]," according to Mamela. "Champions coordinate with their colleagues each day, ensuring that everyone is aware of who is arriving, how we need to prepare their rooms, who is already in-house, and who is departing. Champions are accountable for the program's continuity and execution."

Often when business leaders dream up a new strategy, they are lulled into concluding, "All they [the folks at the front lines] need to do is to *implement* our plan." They forget that the devil is in the details. Richardson and Mamela didn't make that mistake. They recognized that their strategy needed a name and a face, with cross-functional authority, to make sure what's expected got done every time a President's Club member stayed at one of Fairmont's hotels. Creating a champion, instead of sticking the local GM with another new initiative from headquarters, has made all the difference.

In a dismal period for the hospitality industry, Fairmont's President's Club members are staying loyal—room nights booked by members increased 30 percent in 2003, revenues were up 43 percent, and customer-satisfaction ratings have hit new highs. And that's without bribing members with bonus points, give-a-ways, or massive discounting. It's an impressive accomplishment for a mid-sized competitor in a cutthroat industry.

The lesson learned at Fairmont Hotels and Resorts is obvious—follow-through needs a champion. *But how can executives find the right person to be a champion?*

Most bosses appoint an ambitious manager who's already part of the team. But it's not enough. In this chapter, you'll learn what to do to match the right champion in your organization to your goals: what to look for and what to avoid when you're conducting your initial screening of the candidates. And from one remarkable manager, you'll learn what the attitudes and behaviors are that help champions succeed.

FINDING A CHAMPION

To paraphrase Henry Ford, deciding who should champion the follow-through for an initiative is a lot like deciding who should sing tenor for the opera . . . the person who can sing tenor, of course. But while operatic directors have a criterion for evaluating who can and cannot sing tenor, there's no similar checklist for auditioning the candidates for champion.

So Mario Garcia created one.

Dr. Garcia is the founder and CEO of Garcia Media, a design consulting company that helps newspapers, magazines, and other graphic media publishers redesign and refocus their publications. Redesigning a newspaper is a tough job. Get it right and a paper will attract and hold the attention of more readers, making the publication more valuable to its advertisers. But create the wrong look, and a newspaper puts itself at financial risk, as readers and advertisers defect. In a world of desktop access to streaming news, scores of twenty-four-hour cable TV stations, and radical changes in the public's information tastes, Garcia's seventy-two design experts help keep many revered print media companies from becoming stale and losing money.

"A redesign is usually divided into four stages—the briefing, the initial creative push, concessions to reality, and implementation," Garcia explained. "Those early stages typically get 150 percent of everyone's attention, which is great. But the real work starts later, after the executives and key personnel have turned their focus back to their day-to-day concerns."

That sounds like what happens in the life of most new initiatives. It's exciting to go off on a retreat and dream up answers to the question "What would you change if you had a magic wand and could do anything to make your business better?" It's invigorating to throw in your two cents and have everybody hear how creative or insightful you can be. Everyone lines up to participate.

When it comes time for following through, however, a lot of participants have "other, more important" priorities.

Garcia knew a successful redesign would hinge on having someone who would enthusiastically champion the hard part of the project. "The most successful projects are those where one person is responsible," Garcia said.

He also knew that the job took different skills from those of a visionary. "[The champion's] real protagonist role starts in phase three [concessions to reality] and continues through to the end," Garcia said. "I see him or her as a locomotive engineer. She keeps the train on track with enough oil, fuel, and water to last the scheduled journey."

So Garcia set out to discover what skills were critical and what kinds of people were right for the job of champion.

In the beginning, Garcia's clients would select the project leader (whom he dubbed "Mr./Ms. Follow-Through"). "The board of directors or publisher would greet me and say, 'So-and-so here will be taking the changes through the organization,'" he said.

"This seldom worked out," Garcia realized. "It was clear [to me] that not everybody was up to the challenge."

So Garcia began keeping track of the best champions among his many projects. From analyzing those with nearly flawless follow-through to those for whom he had to spend a lot of time fixing the follow-through himself, Garcia created a six-point checklist, a directory of the attitudes and behaviors that quickly identify the person with the best potential to succeed as a champion. Using his checklist, Garcia Media was able to sort through everyone on staff and help locate the person with the most potential before the end of phase one. If that person wasn't the client's predetermined project leader, Garcia's people negotiated a change before the redesign activities began.

What are the six points Garcia uses to audition candidates for Mr. or Ms. Follow-Through?

1. The champion must have a high degree of empathy.

As we covered in "Read Between the Lines," empathy, or the ability to recognize feelings, thoughts, and experiences of another *without* necessarily having those feelings, communicated in an objective or explicit manner, is an extremely valuable management skill. That's especially true of a champion.

"Let me give you an example," Garcia said. "Usually the top brass wants to [personally] approve every change. But it's often impossible to get them all together for a group approval." The easy solution, for many project leaders, is to set a firm schedule and simply let those in attendance at a meeting make the final decision.

Lots of people run things with a "if you snooze, you lose" attitude. In other words, the way they keep things moving and everyone on track is to be tough on all the participants. "If you can't make time to be available for approvals and respond in a timely manner, then your opinion shouldn't count" is their message.

"But," Garcia continued, "we saw that when you leave one decision maker out of the loop, he or she would often later reject that change, or another unrelated change, *simply because their feelings were hurt over being excluded.*

"One of my best Ms. Follow-Throughs was always very good at anticipating the reactions of others. If one of the key people was not in the meeting, she would say, 'I think we have 90 percent of a decision, but we will not have 100 percent until so-and-so sees this.' Then she made sure they saw it."

By putting herself in their shoes and realizing they might resent not being accommodated, that champion created extra work for herself. But by publicly showing that every executive's input would be respected, she told the top brass their status would be protected. That peace of mind generated more cooperation and a willingness to make time for quick turnarounds and approvals. In the end, she created less work and streamlined the process.

So look for empathy when selecting a champion.

2. The champion asks a lot of logistics-related questions like "Can you give me a time frame?" or "What's next?"

"The right person *needs* to keep track of what is due tomorrow at 8 A.M. and next Thursday at 6 P.M.," Garcia said. "They are worried about potential conflicts and insist that all the handoffs are clear and understood. They have the ability to see the mission [as a whole] and at the same time every small detail and its effect [on getting things done]."

They also need the kind of conscientiousness to worry about what might get in the way of the process, working to be proactive rather than reactive. Some leaders consider logistics to be too mundane for their visionary brains. They'd be a poor choice to champion any follow-through.

Look for someone who can sense the proper sequence in any big accomplishment and has shown the ability to see around corners.

3. The right person is a great multitasker.

During any change initiative, the champion might have four top priorities and eighteen people to juggle. They must work like the performer from the old TV variety shows, who could keep twenty-four plates spinning on twenty-four sticks, going up and down the row, giving each plate just enough attention to keep it from falling until the next pass.

"The best people keep their heads [and their poise] during complex and uncertain situations," Garcia discovered, "maintaining a strong sense of direction and purpose."

Don't let someone who has to put blinders on or who loses their temper when they are asked to juggle priorities be your champion.

Look for someone who can juggle like a pro.

4. Champions need to be straight shooters.

Sometimes the champion needs to take the bull by the horns.

For example, one champion approached Garcia an hour before a big meeting and said, "Mario, I think you need to edit your presentation." She saw from Garcia's notes that he would go on too long and lose the attention of several key executives. So she told him (in no uncertain terms) to make a change.

This was a young woman working on her first redesign telling a man with thirty-one years of experience and an international list of successful redesigns that his planned speech was not appropriate and that he needed to fix it. That took nerve. This champion didn't avoid the issue or defer to Garcia's greater experience. She tackled it head-on.

"When the right person [for champion] talks to you, he or she looks you right in the eye," said Garcia. That takes emotional stability, strength, and self-confidence. Being up front and direct when necessary is crucial for gaining trust.

Candidates who are shy, inhibited, or passive-aggressive are a bad choice.

5. Champions feel more satisfaction from the team's accomplishments than their own.

Some of the best organizational wisdom comes from the writings of Lao-Tzu. In 600 B.C., he wrote the following about champions and their accomplishments:

> When the Master governs, the people are hardly aware he exists. When his work is done, his people say, "Amazing, we did it all by ourselves!"

Not getting recognized for their contribution bothers a lot of leaders. They need to be heralded, congratulated, and have their egos stroked. Some are so insecure they actually steal credit away from their associates. That might be fine for boardroom posturing, but it's not for champions at the front lines. Follow-through requires a lot of invisible collaboration; managers on ego trips ruin the spirit that drives collaboration.

The right champion must, Garcia said, "let the project be king and put themselves aside." They need enough self-esteem to be incredibly generous with giving credit, making sure each team member can see their fingerprints on the final product. And they need to be secure enough to forget about *getting* credit.

6. The right person has to be willing to learn new skills.

"Nobody comes ready to lead the follow-through," Garcia said. "Business schools don't prepare them and most on-the-job experience doesn't prepare them. The reason most people are where they are in management is they were the best salesperson, engineer, accountant, or reporter." They have a high degree of technical proficiency, but they have no training in what it takes to get others to follow through.

Yale professor of psychology Carol Dweck has discovered a couple of traits that can help you identify someone who will have problems learning new things.

If a person acts like they believe that "mistakes mean I'm stupid," or if they show that one of their top priorities is looking good to others, he or she will have a hard time learning new things.*

*Guy Claxton, *Wise Up: The Challenge of Lifelong Learning*, Bloomsbury Publishing, 1999.

The right potential champion will show an ease in confronting mistakes and learning from them.

Garcia agrees. "The worst choice is someone who is using the project to build their reputation or climb to the next position," he said. "These people are too concerned about how they look."

PUTTING THE CRITERIA TO WORK

According to Garcia, while redesigns are a highly technical process, the champion doesn't need a lot of technical skills. The hardest part of the job isn't making the right technical decisions. The hardest part, Garcia said, "is the human condition. That, at the end of the day, determines . . . [if the follow-through] succeeds or fails."

In other words, choosing a champion is a matter of hiring the right attitudes over technical experience.

In the chapter "Hire Attitudes Over Experience," we learned how the Big Five dimensions of personality—conscientiousness, openness, agreeableness, extroversion, and emotional stability—help create a profile of "right attitudes." Use the same process to identify your champion.

First look over Garcia's six criteria, which I introduced on page 58. Next, match the person's personality traits against those criteria by ranking each of the Big Five dimensions of personality on a scale of 1 to 7 to determine the role each will play in fulfilling your goals. Then conduct interviews that uncover the behaviors that demonstrate the candidate has the right degree of those traits.

Remember to look for incidents that will reveal personal traits. Ask the candidate to tell you about a time when they faced those circumstances, how they handled it, and what they would do differently now. Watch out for the clues that indicate someone would be a bad fit—like the inability to multitask or a tendency to hoard the credit for achievements. It's just as important to recognize the clues that someone would make a bad fit as it is to see their good qualities.

Remember Garcia's final point: Championing follow-through requires *learning new skills*. Instead of looking for experience, *ask* about experiences. Uncover the person's attitudes, then figure out if your candidate can learn from mistakes.

In the next section, the person Dr. Garcia called his "icon of follow-through" explains what she did. Her observations should help you finish your template for choosing the right champion.

LEARNING FROM A CHAMPION

In early 2000, Dow Jones & Company decided to redesign and refocus their flagship publication, the *Wall Street Journal*. "The paper had gotten bigger and bigger," a deputy managing editor explained. "This was a chance for everybody to take a step back and answer some questions like 'What should we be doing here? Are we doing something because it's the right thing to do or because we've always done it that way?' Our [redesign] was about making the paper more useful to our readers."

Garcia Media was hired to work alongside the *Journal*'s art director, Joe Dizney, and one of the paper's deputy managing editors, Joanne Lipman. Lipman had helped create *Weekend Journal*, a new section that had been added to the Friday edition of the *Wall Street Journal* in 1998. Getting *Weekend Journal* up and running had taught Lipman how to get bureau chiefs, executives, and boards of directors at both the *Wall Street Journal* and Dow Jones & Company to do their part in following through. Garcia noticed Lipman immediately and began to match this deputy editor to his six criteria for choosing a champion.

Lipman matched up well. She asked Garcia many logistics-related questions and took notes from the beginning. She also looked Garcia and his people right in the eye when she made an observation or asked for a clarification. Lipman told him in early conversation that she "loved blank-slate kinds of projects" and that she didn't take on responsibilities just to advance her career.

But what caught Garcia's eye most of all was Lipman's winning way with people at every level. "We gave each other nicknames," he recalled. "I, of course was Ricky Ricardo because of my Cuban accent. Joanne was quickly called Mary Tyler Moore, because in the show Mary was the one who could turn the world on with her smile." Lipman had the same quality. As Garcia said, "She was so sure of herself, but never a threat. People really responded to her."

From interviews it became clear Lipman's stellar manner consisted of more than an experienced reporter's skill at listening or a talented executive's deft touch with people. She came to the project with a passion for her company, her colleagues, and her readers. Lipman clearly loves being a part of the *Wall Street Journal*. And as corny as it might sound, it's her love that caused her to become such an excellent champion of follow-through.

LOVE IS (ALMOST) ALL YOU NEED

Lipman underscored the connection between enthusiasm and being a great champion.

- When asked why she took on the redesign, she replied, "I *love* consensus kinds of projects. I *love* working with a blank slate." Many managers abhor the rigors of creating consensus and are uncomfortable exploring uncharted territory. Lipman looked forward to those challenges.
- When asked about dealing with all the differing opinions and conflicts as she worked through the long process of a total redesign, Lipman said, "I really believe there's a ton of smart people [at the paper], and I *love* hearing what they have to say." Many managers don't respect their associates (or even their bosses) enough to hear their opinions. With Lipman, her passion translated into shows of respect and actions that kept many diverse personalities engaged.
- When asked how she kept everyone happy even during the difficult times, when deadlines loomed, she said, "After I nagged them, I showered them with *love*, of course." People respond to appreciation. It's amazing how many managers fail to practice it. And Lipman's passion took the sting out of tough times.

"You have to *love* what you do," Lipman concluded. "People come to me [when they are offered a new assignment or promotion] and ask, 'Is this a good move for me?' I say, 'It's only a good move if you love doing it.' If you're not going to be happy doing something, if you don't love it . . . it's a terrible move."

This kind of enthusiasm should be the first criterion you look for

in choosing someone to champion your follow-through. Ask yourself, "Can they embrace this project, the people, and love making
sure what's expected gets done?" If you can't see the capacity for
passion from your prospective champion, you'd better keep looking.

Love is *almost* all you need. Besides passion, Lipman showed
three essential skills as she championed follow-through at the *Wall
Street Journal*:

1. The ability to create consensus
2. Showing respect
3. Generating urgency

1. Creating Consensus

Donna didn't enjoy the process of trying to create consensus.

Donna was the director of a billion-dollar buying group, representing about fifty businesses in retail. Buying groups negotiate
deeper discounts for the group by combining everyone's purchases
and making larger commitments to manufacturers.

Sometimes Donna's negotiations matched the individual agendas of all fifty members perfectly. But when a deal wasn't a 100 percent perfect fit, many members followed through halfheartedly,
giving Donna lame excuses when they dropped the ball.

Donna was frustrated. "Our group isn't cohesive," she said. "When
a deal is struck, everybody needs to get behind it. I spend half my life
explaining every detail and coaxing them to participate."

"Isn't there some kind of *enforcement mechanism* groups can use
to force everybody to follow through?" she asked.

Lots of managers feel the same as Donna. They secretly wish for
the days when employees knew their duty was to be obedient, to
accept decisions unquestioningly. That way, the leader could move
on to more important things instead of working so hard to get
everyone to agree.

Lipman didn't share this attitude. She shook off any suggestion
that consensus was more trouble than it was worth. She knew consensus was something that makes for better planning and decision
making. She loved the idea that "everyone wanted to be heard" and

wasn't frustrated at all that others had "their own ideas," which she had to work hard to bring together.

"You still have your vision," she advised, "but you have to have a very open mind about how that vision can be achieved. You can't get your ego wrapped up in this." She has learned that "you get the best ideas" when you solicit everyone's input. And she enjoyed the challenge of fitting all the pieces together. "[I love seeing] where all those comments and all those ideas fit into the grander vision," Lipman said.

Garcia gives a prime example of the difference between someone who is good at creating consensus and those who aren't. "Instead of saying, 'We're going to do this,' Lipman would ask, 'What does everybody think about this?'" he observed.

What to Look For.

Lipman offered her own insights on what it takes to create consensus. You might want to use her criteria when you are evaluating your own candidates for follow-through champion.

Consensus starts with listening.

"Everybody had a role in shaping the decisions," Lipman said of the redesign project at the *Journal.* "I talked to all the bureau chiefs and tons of editors and reporters. . . . The Washington bureau chief had a million ideas. He had a totally different point of view than the people in L.A., who had a different point of view than the 'money and investing' group."

Can your candidate listen? As noted earlier, listening is not the same as not talking. Check with past associates of your candidate; see if they felt listened to and understood. Lots of people make a show of listening but are so wrapped up in their own opinions they don't hear what's been said.

Consensus comes when everyone feels safe enough to speak up.

"People need to know they can go out on a limb and they won't be embarrassed," according to Lipman. "They need to know it's okay to speak up." One way Lipman demonstrated this skill was by carefully balancing the attendance at meetings.

Garcia remembered that Lipman knew instinctively whom to

invite and whom to exclude: "She would say, 'If you invite these two, *this one* will dominate.' She always worried about face-saving."

"You want to keep it a pure experience," Lipman advised. "Meetings or informal get-togethers shouldn't get polluted by things that have nothing to do with what you are working on."

Can your candidate control a group so everyone feels safe to speak up? Do they have the patience to draw out the less articulate people and keep the dominating talkers from taking over? Do they understand that great verbal skills bear no correlation to knowing what you're talking about?

Consensus is fueled by excitement.

The biggest issue around the redesign of the *Wall Street Journal* wasn't keeping the intricate schedules or avoiding conflicts in priorities. According to Lipman, it was keeping people inspired and excited. "You [have to] start with your own sense of enthusiasm," she said.

Lipman fueled everyone's excitement by making sure they felt they were making a contribution. "You make sure everybody feels like, 'I see my fingerprints on that.' People get excited when they have a piece of the whole idea and you show them how it's been woven into something larger."

Lipman was very generous, showering participants with praise and letting everyone know how much this was a collaboration.

Can your candidate get others excited? Is he or she generally optimistic? What have they done to maintain excitement over long periods? Can they accept this responsibility or will they blame any lack of excitement on others and external events?

2. Showing Respect

During the redesign process, Lipman showed a lot of respect by sharing the proposed redesign not just to bosses but to the folks who would be affected by it.

For example, she included the Page One editor in the approval process, even though he wasn't a part of the hierarchy. "Before we showed the changes to the executives, I thought it was important to show it to the Page One editor," she recalled. "We were working on his proprietary interest. This was his baby. We shouldn't spring it on him after others have gone through it and signed off. So we brought him in quietly (we were doing this all in secret) and gave him a preview."

Now, that's a great show of respect for a busy champion on a tight deadline.

Many leaders aren't skilled at balancing getting things done and showing respect. (There's an entire chapter devoted to the subject later in this book in Building Block IV, "Individual Initiative.")

Garcia believes you must look for someone who is very sensitive. "I say you need [someone with a] 10 percent fear factor to lead the follow-through," he said. "[A champion] needs a fear of hurt feelings, a fear of somebody being left out."

Lipman showed her respect for everyone by taking time to explain and sharing the credit.

Explaining is a show of respect.

The courtesy of a good explanation is the first casualty of tight deadlines. "We don't have time," hurried managers plead. "Why can't they just trust me?"

Lipman learned intelligent people are far more trusting after you give them good explanations. "Everyone is going to be impacted, even if their ideas don't end up being a part of the final project," Lipman said of the redesign initiative. They want to be kept in the loop.

For example, with the top brass, Lipman would tell them how she'd decided on each step that was taken. "I found bosses especially wanted to hear about the development," she said. "You want them to go through the process, explain the thinking behind it." Those explanations built trust.

Has your candidate got the patience to explain things to many different people many different ways? Do they feel the need to stay engaged, or is it a bother?

Giving credit to others is a show of respect.

"When people make a contribution, everybody should know

about it," Lipman said. "I get that from my boss, Paul Steiger [the managing editor of the *Wall Street Journal*]. He's always making sure others are getting the credit. I don't believe in collecting everybody's ideas and putting my name on them." Giving credit is a show of respect for the group's contribution.

Quiz your candidate on their accomplishments. Who else do they give credit to? Are they generous? Have others ever felt cheated out of rightful credit? Does that bother your candidate?

3. Generating Urgency

In the parable of the Frog in the Pot (from Peter Senge's *The Fifth Discipline*), if you put a frog in a pot of really hot water it will immediately try to scramble out. But if you start with a frog in a pot of room-temperature water, he'll settle in the pan. As you apply heat and the water temperature goes from warm to very warm and all the way to hot, the frog will remain in the water until he becomes frog soup. Why? Because the gradual nature of change doesn't register until it's too late. Peter Senge's frog needed a champion to say, "Haven't you noticed? The water was room temperature at the start, but now it's turned quite steamy. If this continues, you might get cooked."

Somebody needs to *give* your frog a sense of urgency.

Some people call creating urgency nagging. But it's doubtful that the frog would have considered the person who awoke him from his lethargy and focused his attention on the impending danger a nag. You wouldn't either.

Everybody needs some nagging now and then. The only pertinent question for a champion is "How should the nagging be handled?"

Nobody at the *Wall Street Journal* minded Lipman's nagging. Her sensitivity to their feelings and natural good nature helped her develop rules for keeping her nagging from being intolerable.

Do it in doses.

Lipman had to pick her battles and remember that her priorities were not the only priority for those around her. "Everyone has a job with its own deadlines, and your project is just one more thing," she reminded herself.

Make concessions to reality.

"If someone says, 'Wait a minute, we can't possibly . . .' or 'Please, you're asking me to do too much,' you have to really listen," Lipman advised. Successful nags are sensitive about asking for too much and being unrealistic.

Have more than one way of nagging.

Staying in someone's face and putting your own work at the top of their list takes versatility. "Sometimes you have to beg and cajole," Lipman said. Other times she just laid it out straight: "Okay, guys, by the end of the week we have to finish these five things." Everyone responds differently, depending on the situation.

Use positive reinforcement.

"When they come through for you, you really have to show them you appreciate them," Lipman advised. "You have to do something nice, reward them. Mario's trick was to take us out to lunch and buy champagne. Sometimes you have to buy people presents. I showered them with love, of course."

Ask your candidate to describe a situation where they had to nag a boss and a situation where they had to nag a subordinate to get things done. Look for them to describe how they demonstrated a deft touch. Ask yourself, "Could this person nag me without my minding it?"

Champion is an especially appropriate word for the person chosen to lead a follow-through. It comes from the thirteenth century, meaning a gladiator, militant advocate, or defender, one who does battle for another's interests (a *champion* of civil rights). Champions are passionate battlers fighting inattention, distractions, lethargy on the inside, and all external obstructions from the outside to make sure what's expected gets done.

Keep that image in your mind as you look to a candidate (or in the mirror) and ask, "Can you champion the follow-through?"

Building Block III

■

BUY-IN

Now that you've read about how to give your people a crystal clear direction and how to match the right employees to every goal, you're nearly ready to start following through. That's right: *nearly ready*.

All managers have heard the sorry tale of the bright idea that got away. Everyone loved the strategy initially, the story goes, as it was sure to resolve some nagging problem or capitalize on a significant opportunity. But the brilliant initiative never saw the light of day, or if it did get started, it quickly stalled and then fell apart. All that was left in its wake were feelings of loss and confusion.

These stories are all punctuated with the same fact—anyone with a reasonably open mind could see the idea was destined to make things better. "Why," managers were left to wonder, "didn't we follow through?"

Why? Because, no matter how clear your expectations are or how well your people are matched to their personal and their division's goals, following through always includes a *change* in direction. As Isaac Newton explained three centuries ago, all objects (people included) resist any change in direction until you apply enough force to break them free from the law of inertia.

In business, the force that breaks an organization free from its inertia is called *buy-in*.

Buy-in is management shorthand for an associate's willingness to trust and go in new or unfamiliar directions and do his or her best to help others on the team follow through.

It's readily apparent when a team has buy-in. Associates approach each day with optimism and openness—quickly adapting to unexpected events, improvising solutions on the spot, and extending the extra effort necessary to overcome small roadblocks. Teams that *buy in* support the group's goals and each other—coaching, assisting, and encouraging everyone on the team to follow through.

It's also obvious when a team doesn't buy in. Negativity and resistance (rather than optimism and openness) can be sensed in the air—people drag their feet, chronically complain about everything, and point their fingers at someone else whenever things don't go as planned. Teams that don't buy in become dysfunctional—with a few associates working behind the leader's back to sabotage those who are trying to follow though.

Conventional wisdom says that if your reasons for changing direction are well communicated and your plan is solid, the majority of people will buy in automatically. At the most, that conventional wisdom continues, if their buy-in isn't automatic, managers can get enough buy-in by giving their teams a chance to *participate* in deciding what is to be done.

But that line of thinking doesn't match up to reality. More often than not, no matter how well a leader communicates the reasons, or how intelligently he plans, or even how much participation he facilitates, *not* buying in is the automatic reaction to new or unfamiliar directions.

So managers need the skills for starting the implementation of every bright idea and change in direction with more buy-in— enough to break their teams free from the law of inertia. That's the purpose of this third building block.

7 OUTMANEUVER THE CAVE PEOPLE

The single, most powerful piece of advice for overcoming the law of inertia and thereby improving your organization's follow-through can be summed up in four words: *outmaneuver the CAVE people*.

In this context, CAVE stands for "citizens against virtually everything."*

Just as our bodies have an immune system that assaults everything new and unfamiliar, organizations have their own autoimmune response that instinctively and impulsively attacks every new idea, novel solution, and call for change. Overtly and covertly, these antibodies in human form (aka the CAVE people) chip away at your team's willingness to trust and try new things, poisoning the environment in order to keep necessary changes from taking hold.

As a result of their assault on buy-in, your team's follow-through gets fractured and the bright idea or necessary change in direction slips through the cracks.

Like doctors preparing a patient for a transplant, managers must take steps to outmaneuver the inevitable onslaught by the CAVE

*Thanks to Anand Sharma of TBM Consulting Group for the acronym.

people. These steps must be planned and implemented before your team can begin to follow through.

In this chapter, you'll learn how to neutralize the CAVE people's opposition to new ideas and different ways of doing things. We'll formulate a plan to both promote and protect your team's buy-in and the tactics that will thwart every predictable attack from your company's CAVE people.

To begin, let's make sure this threat is fresh in your mind. Take a look how the CAVE people opposed the necessary changes at Home Depot.

TRANSFORMING HOME DEPOT

When a rock star with a top-selling CD doesn't sell as many of his next recording, people are usually surprised. They shouldn't be. The rock star is experiencing a common phenomenon called "regression toward the mean." Regression is a statistical observation that says "extreme experiences tend to get balanced by less extreme experiences."

In business, regression means that no intelligent executive should expect their phenomenal success to last forever. The only way to remain an above-average performer is for leaders to transform their organizations—changing and improving the way they do things to escape the pull of mediocrity.

Home Depot has been a rock star of the business world. Arthur Blank and Bernard Marcus started a small, three-store group in 1979 and cranked out the equivalent of twenty-one hit records over twenty-one years. They opened more than 1,300 successful stores and went from nothing to $53 billion in sales. Profits grew an average of 35 percent every year in the 1990s. If you bought one hundred shares of stock when Home Depot first went public, those shares were worth $1.6 million dollars after that incredible run. To put their company's track record of phenomenal success in perspective, since 1985 fewer than forty companies of the Fortune 1000 have performed as well as Home Depot.

But by early 2000, Home Depot's sales growth had started to slow and profits followed. Inventories became bloated, management appeared to lose focus, and the company's stock price dropped by 33 percent. A new competitor (Lowe's) began closing the gap between themselves and America's leading home-improvement retailer.

Home Depot's board rightly saw this as a sign that the company's unparalleled record of success and therefore its above-average returns to shareholders were in danger of regressing. They called a meeting and asked investment banker and Home Depot board member Ken Langone to look around for a new CEO, someone who could help the company transform itself and get back to cranking out the hits.

He came back with a terrific candidate named Bob Nardelli.

Nardelli had spent thirty years at General Electric, putting in more hours, tackling the toughest assignments, and showing he was, as then CEO Jack Welch declared, the "best operating executive [at GE]." He had transformed both GE Transportation and GE Power Systems, increasing profits at GE Power Systems nearly 700 percent in five years.*

Langone thought Nardelli's experience with the ins and outs of changing already successful businesses, as well as his intimate knowledge of the processes and disciplines at one of the world's most respected large organizations, would help Home Depot get back to delivering above-average results fast. The board agreed and Nardelli was hired.

Nardelli started by making all the right moves—he asked a lot of questions and analyzed the strengths and weaknesses of the market, the organization, and its culture. He set a stretch goal—to double sales and more than double profits by 2005—and laid out a strategy that was specific, measurable, accountable, realistic, and time-bound (SMART).

He communicated this strategy through town hall and individual meetings, introducing proven new disciplines that would dramatically improve purchasing, operations, human resources, and management systems. He emphasized the good sense behind all these changes in simple, clear terms everyone could understand. "We have to change the business model," he said. "What got Home

*Patricia Sellers, "Something to Prove," *Fortune* magazine, June 24, 2002.

Depot to the first $50 billion [in sales] won't get us to the second $50 billion." And then Nardelli rolled up his sleeves and asked the teams at Home Depot to join him in following through.

INSEAD University professor Spyros Makridakis writes that executives (like Nardelli) are up against enormous odds: "For every successful corporate turnaround, there are two that fail," he states.* Why? "Organizational resistance to change," Makridakis concludes, is a bigger challenge than most managers are prepared to face.

Take a look at the resistance Nardelli faced.

THE "CAVE PEOPLE" HAVE THEIR SAY

Just as associates were beginning to implement Nardelli's strategic changes, Home Depot's customer enthusiasm sagged to new lows, sales slowed even more, and its share price declined further. Predictably, this gave the company's "CAVE people"—the citizens against virtually everything Nardelli wanted to change—the ammunition they needed to assault Home Depot's new direction.

- CAVE people in the stores started whispering, "Nardelli has no retail background" and "The board is paying him too much money."
- "Everything he's doing is counterculture," one of the many former senior executives told *BusinessWeek* (Nardelli replaced 24 of 39 top officers in his first 19 months in an effort to make sure he had the *right* people). "He's bad for morale." A former corporate trainer chimed in, "There's nowhere near the passion as there was under the old guard."
- Midlevel CAVE managers carped about Nardelli's command-and-control manner. "Things weren't presented to you," said a store executive, "they were told to you." And others squawked that Nardelli didn't appreciate the magic of the Home Depot way. "He doesn't get it," they grumbled as they begged their old boss, Bernie Marcus, to come back and run the company.
- Wall Street analysts added to the negativity. "The market's getting saturated," one analyst wrote (even though Home Depot

---

*Spyros G. Makridakis, *Forecasting, Planning and Strategy for the 21st Century*, The Free Press, 1990.

had only about a 10 percent market share). "I wouldn't be in a rush to buy it [Home Depot's stock]," concluded another.

- One former merchandising executive gave everyone the ultimate illogical argument to categorically reject Nardelli's carefully thought-out change in direction. "On paper all those changes made sense," he said in an interview with the *Wall Street Journal*. "Unfortunately, they don't work on the floor of the stores."

Every manager who has ever initiated new ideas has seen this same reaction; any announced change that's followed by even the slightest negative news brings a chorus of "Retreat!" from anonymous staff and other armchair observers. Because of Home Depot's size and reputation as a rock star in the business world, all the CAVE-person grousing got a lot of public attention. *The Economist* wrote a headline that labeled Nardelli's necessary changes "a do-it-yourself disaster." The *Wall Street Journal* followed with its own negative headline, "A Hardware Chain Struggles to Adjust . . . Employees Squawk." *Fortune* magazine asked glumly in a headline, "Can Home Depot Get Its Groove Back?"

Those negative headlines were published in the first quarter of 2003, two years after Nardelli took charge. Still, it was way too early to connect Nardelli's change in direction to the more bad news in same-store sales or declines in market value. After all, Home Depot had been stalling as the new CEO arrived. You don't need a degree in physics to realize that there's always a delay between implementation of a change in course and the results of that change. Any of these short-term bad outcomes could have been the trailing effect of a situation created long before Nardelli instituted his transformation plan.

The bad press for Home Depot was nothing more than an extension of the "CAVE people's spin machine," which every manager should anticipate will attack their requests for follow-through.

- The CAVE people attacked the man rather than the validity of his plan. ("Nardelli has no retail background. He's making too much money. He's bringing in a bunch of GE cronies.")
- The CAVE people used "facts" that sounded bad but could not be checked for cause-and-effect links. ("There's nowhere near the

passion. Morale is down. Unfortunately, they [Nardelli's changes] don't work on the floor of the stores.")

- And the CAVE people suggested that because sales slumped and investors bailed after he started, Nardelli was the reason. (One fundamental in all CAVE-person arguments is ignoring coincidences and refusing to factor in the time it takes for causes to produce their intended effect. CAVE people like to suggest, "It happened after you made your change—therefore, it was caused by the change you made.")

Through their barrage of negative spin, the CAVE people fueled a strong emotional argument designed to thwart Nardelli's actions at Home Depot: *This new strategy looks risky. Let's wait and see.*

CAVE people know in their bones that if they can convince enough people to drag their feet—through calls for caution, increased suspicion about management's motives, and eloquently stated but completely invalid reasoning—the combined resistance will delay any changes from taking hold and ultimately fracture the team's follow-through. Their hope is that buy-in will fall through the cracks and things will continue in the old direction.

Most managers underestimate the power of the CAVE people's spin. They think that the obvious need for a change, their careful planning, and good communications will counter this negativity. These managers forget the truth of the human condition. A CAVE person's attack is not founded on reason. It is an emotional appeal to people's fear of change and the comfortable pull of the law of inertia. Remember, *You cannot reason a person out of a position they did not reason themselves into.*

The only solution is to accurately anticipate the emotional frailty of the human condition and outmaneuver those CAVE people.

DID NARDELLI HAVE WHAT HE NEEDED?

Let's consider a few key questions:

- Did Nardelli accurately diagnose what he was up against in changing Home Depot's "loosey-goosey" culture?
- Did he select his first battles with an eye toward neutralizing the CAVE people's negative spin?

- Did he create enough in-house disciples to counter the CAVE people at work in each of Home Depot's many locations?
- Did he make sure the people at the top (in his case, the board of directors and stockholders) could *taste and feel* enough progress to ignore the CAVE people from Wall Street?

In other words, did Nardelli have what is needed to outmaneuver the CAVE people?

Probably not, is Nardelli's own assessment. "I may have underestimated how challenging the implementation would be," he admitted to Wall Street as he sharply lowered analysts' expectations two years into his follow-through. (As of the summer of 2004, Home Depot remains about $30 billion dollars short of its 2005 target and the share price is still down almost 50 percent.)

Don't underestimate how challenging your implementation will be. You now know that two-thirds of all changes in direction fail and that organizational resistance (a lack of buy-in caused by the attacks of the CAVE people) is a big reason why.

Anand Sharma has put together a simple four-step strategy any manager (at any level) can use to outmaneuver the CAVE people and get the buy-in they need to successfully follow through.

SHARMA'S STRATEGY

Anand Sharma leads eighty-eight experts in North America, South America, and Europe at one of the most successful change consultancies in the world, TBM Consulting Group.

TBM's mission is to help clients change direction and "get lean." "Lean" is shorthand in manufacturing circles for changing a company's existing processes to decrease lead times, lower inventory levels, and improve productivity dramatically. When a company "gets lean," it becomes a much better competitor—efficiency is boosted, profits go up, and both customers and employees are happier.

For example, TBM client The Lantech Company was a $39-million company experiencing significant losses when they first got in touch with Sharma. After Lantech "got lean," they skyrocketed, turning into a $90-million business. Amazingly, it was all accomplished with about *the same number of employees.*

During the decade that Pella Corporation has worked with TBM, they have seen their net margins double and a 65 percent decrease in lead times. Pella's sales have gone up 250 percent, and they were recognized by *Fortune* magazine as one of the best places in America to work.

First Data (a division of Western Union) is currently working with TBM to reduce lead times in their business by 70 to 90 percent and grow their revenues and profits by millions of dollars. TBM has helped more than five hundred manufacturers like these lift productivity an average of 15 to 20 percent a year.

Yet despite TBM's platinum track record (they have a 98 percent client-retention rate) and the significant improvements they make in their client's bottom line, Sharma never begins a project underestimating the organizational resistance to the changes in direction required by the lean methodologies. TBM always begins with a strategy to outmaneuver the company's CAVE people. "I work very hard to neutralize their negativity," he said.

"Every organization needs very, very strong motivating reasons to do difficult things," Sharma said. "We have to melt away any resistance . . . and have the team experience dramatic change before their company's CAVE people are able to mount a fight."

Sharma shared four steps he's proven can outmaneuver the CAVE people and result in more buy-in:

1. Kick off your change with a "wow!" event.
2. Blitzkrieg them (blitzkrieg means to follow through so fast the CAVE people don't have the time to organize their resistance).
3. Create disciples from the rank and file.
4. Take your success story straight to the top.

KICK OFF THINGS WITH A "WOW!" EVENT

Just as a wildfire expert intentionally sets a blaze in advance of the forest fire, outmaneuvering the CAVE people starts by preparing to fight fire with fire.

CAVE people will inevitably use negative spin to "sell" people on dragging their feet and not following through. Kicking off your change with a "wow!" event generates positive spin so you're able to neutralize that negativity.

"Everyone's first experience is a defining moment," Sharma explained. "Ten years later, those people will say, 'I remember that first time—lights flashed and everyone went, wow!' That 'wow!' factor is very important for overcoming the challenges and negativity. *'Wow!'* will get one to do very difficult things," Sharma said.

Sharma still remembers the wow when he first implemented the lessons of the Toyota Production System. "It was 1979 and I was working at American Standard as director of Manufacturing Services. I had just heard Dr. Shigeo Shingo [the originator with Taiichi Ohno of the lean methodologies at Toyota] speaking at a conference," he remembered. After the session, Dr. Shingo gave Sharma his book and suggested that if Sharma liked his ideas he should try to implement them.

Sharma went back to the American Standard factory in Pittsburgh and did just that. "In one factory, we increased productivity 33 percent and cut inventory from $54 million to $18 million," he said. "Those were some incredible, incredible improvements." In other words, "wow!"

Here's a three-point checklist for making sure your first event has what it takes for your people to say "wow!":

❑ *The results should read like an advertising headline.*

Look to begin with a project that would give you a headline that can capture everyone's attention, as the diet people do when they get a woman to say, "I lost ten pounds in just seven days."

"Let me give you an example," Sharma said. "Lantech [a manufacturer of industrial packaging solutions] needed about two hundred different metal parts to make one [shrink-wrapping] machine, because each had so many variations. Twelve workers were kept busy making all those parts, running up and down."

Sharma told the team assembled to kick off lean strategies at Lantech, "Rather than staying busy making these two hundred components, let's make a kit that makes this—just one at a time."

Sharma knew that if the team found a way to create that kit they would go from twelve people running around down to just two, and he would have his headline: "We achieved an *84 percent* reduction in head count."

So the team went ahead and took a process that required twelve people and found a way to do it, using lean tactics, with just two. Everyone said, "Wow!"

Most organizations just dive into their first project without weighing the "wow!" factor. But that's conceding too much territory to the CAVE people.

An 84 percent reduction in headcount, a million dollars in extra profits, doubling the inventory turn, increasing the average sale by 50 percent—these headline-type results get the "wow!" you need. Before you finalize your next rollout, write the headline based on the goal for your first project and test it for its wow factor.

❑ *The wow event must be biased for success.*

Do you remember Chicken Little? In that story, the chicken gets conked by a tiny acorn and then convinces the hen, goose, duck, and turkey that the sky is falling. The same thing happens in organizations. Every failure is the beginning of a trend, according to a company's CAVE people.

That's why Sharma insists that before his people introduce any lean strategies into an organization, they find a situation that's biased for success, where achieving the desired results is *very likely*. But finding that situation takes a careful diagnosis.

Sharma and his team typically walk the factory floor looking for obvious signs of waste in a manufacturing process—unsynchronized transportation, pointless waiting, unnecessary motion, time wasted fixing preventable defects, overproduction, extra steps in processing, and inventory overloads. "We'll draw a map—where we can find out where are the disconnects, the issues," he noted. "We'll ask, 'What is the heart and soul of this operation?' and 'What's your bread and butter?'"

After this careful analysis, his team will choose the challenge with the best potential success factor.

Most managers are overconfident. They feel they can take on any situation. They forget that the CAVE people are lurking in the shadows, ready to trumpet any glitches as signs that "the sky is falling."

Don't think anyone will appreciate your bravery in testing new ideas when you're up against impossible challenges. And don't think your people will have the character to accept early setbacks. Bosses are the first to follow Chicken Little's lead, and your people are second.

❏ *Keep the CAVE people out of the "wow!" event.*

Bill Zollars (CEO at Yellow Corporation) needed to change the work systems at more than three hundred shipping and receiving depots across America. Each location had enough CAVE people to suffocate his new ideas. So instead of going to the closest depot to roll out his changes, Zollars searched for and zeroed in on the one group friendly to him and his team's discoveries about "best" practices—the Cleveland depot.

Nurtured in a friendly environment (a depot without CAVE people), Zollars's changes took root quickly and flourished. "Cleveland improved throughput [packages per employee] more than 35 percent," Zollars said. "[Their success] led our companywide rollout of a program that gave us more capacity across the entire organization without any capital investment."

As crazy as it sounds, sensible and intelligent managers often tell me during the postmortem of a failed initiative, "I knew so-and-so was going to be a negative influence."

If they knew so-and-so was going to be a disrupter, then *why* did they let her on the team or why did they select her location? It's as if they never learned the lesson of the fox and the scorpion:

> A scorpion was walking along the bank of a river, wondering how he would get to the other side. Suddenly he

saw a fox preparing to swim across. He asked the fox if he would give him a ride on his back.

The fox said, "No—if I let you go with me on my back, you'll sting me and I'll drown."

The scorpion assured him, "If I did that, we'd both drown."

So the fox agreed. The scorpion climbed up on his back and fox began to swim, and half way across the river, the scorpion stung him.

As he felt the sting and the venom began to work, the fox turned to the scorpion and said, "Why did you do that? Now you'll drown too."

"I couldn't help it," said the scorpion. "It's my nature."

The CAVE people are going to poison your "wow!" event—it's in their nature. Never, never, never give them the opportunity.

We went over the tools you need for identifying what kind of people you're dealing with in "Hire Attitudes Over Experience" and "Match Everyone's Agenda." Use those tools to identify the type of attitudes that are typical of a CAVE person. Look for individual agendas that run counter to your change in direction. Interview and analyze the people who will play a role in your first project and then screen out the CAVE people.

BLITZKRIEG THEM

"One of my mentors was [the late] Yoshiki Iwata," Sharma said. "He was one of the first general managers asked to take the methodology [the Toyota Production System] to Toyota's second- and third-tier suppliers. But he was told, 'You don't have twenty-five years [the time it took Toyota to implement the changes.]' It has to be done in five years."

So Iwata came up with the idea of what he called a "kaizen blitzkrieg" (also called "blitz," which is short for blitzkrieg). *Kaizen* is a Japanese word that means "to take apart and put back together in a better way." A blitzkrieg is "a sudden and overpowering attack." Kaizen blitzkrieg, therefore, is "a quick and overpowering effort to take something apart and put it back together in a better way." Iwata's kaizen blitz needs just five days to make a breakthrough in productivity. Using those principles, Iwata was able to implement the Toyota Production System in other companies in 80 percent less time than it took at Toyota.

Sharma noticed another benefit of blitz methods. "They [the CAVE people] are used to getting a lot of attention," Sharma said. "They use eloquent arguments because they have a lot of free time and they aren't accustomed to moving fast."

Kaizen blitz lets Sharma outrun the CAVE people from the get-go.

Sharma gives teams just five days to learn the tools for analyzing processes, observe what's being done, completely redesign the methods to achieve some dramatic improvement, implement the change, and present their results to the CEO.

When the teams hear they have only one day to thoroughly observe every aspect and understand what adds value and what doesn't, they always object. "We need time to study," they tell Sharma.

"No," Sharma tells them, "you don't have time to study." Sharma knows that if they study something for five or six weeks, the CAVE people will have time to convince them not to do anything at all. It's called paralysis by analysis.

Sharma says to the team, "We need you to observe better than you've ever observed in your life. We will teach you how."

"We can help you to develop 'kaizen eyes' and a keen sense of observation to take common sense and mix that with action. We can do that in two hours," Sharma explains. "Then, if we fail, we will have time to redo it."

Every leader who has cracked the code on follow-through has used some element of urgency. One executive called it "taking heavy action"; another said it was having a "pounce" mentality. Bill Zollars gave his people at Yellow Transportation days instead of months to start up their expedited delivery service. John Borthwick's Advanced Services Team at Time Warner went from hearing his boss complain, "Why can't I listen to my e-mail?" to having a prototype for a new service called AOL by Phone in *three* weeks.

It's all about total immersion, learning by doing, and refusing to take a leisurely pace. "It all must be done at such a speed," Sharma said, "CAVE people don't have time to develop an eloquent argument, saying, 'This is not going to work because we are different.' Before they can think up why it won't work, you have results before you."

CREATE ADVOCATES FROM THE RANK AND FILE

By the time the CAVE people see changes taking hold and start to react, the second wave of Sharma's outmaneuver strategy has mobilized. Noting that he won't work with a client without a promise for no layoffs, Sharma said, he recruits certain individuals who've been "liberated" from nonproductive activities to help with the next round of implementations—they might "become part of the kaizen improvement team or go into the pool of people that can be a flex force" to help with absentees and vacations, Sharma explained.

These liberated workers are not the ones with the least seniority or those with the fewest abilities or the least knowledge, Sharma explained. Rather, they're the most senior, most capable, most experienced, most versatile people. They become the team enablers and potential team leaders.

"These people become the ambassadors to carry the positive energy of the kaizen breakthrough to every part of the organization. They are a force of such stature and experience that no CAVE person can say, 'But you don't understand. Things are different.' No opponent can whisper, 'We tried that and it didn't work.' We've made a force to change the culture from *inside* the culture," Sharma explained.

These advocates from the rank and file have the following attributes:

1. They've seen everything work with their own eyes.
2. They know how bad things used to be.
3. They have the insider knowledge to counter the CAVE people's arguments.
4. They can speak from a position of no hidden agenda.

It's a masterstroke. A force of the most experienced and senior employees, extolling the virtues of the transformation and effectively outmaneuvering the CAVE people.

TAKE YOUR STORY STRAIGHT TO THE TOP

Sharma explained the final element of his plan to outmaneuver the CAVE people.

"The project team makes a presentation on what they've done and how they've done it to the most top management," he said.

"You see by day five they are walking on air," Sharma explains. "Standing before the CEO and all the top executives are ten to twelve people from several layers of the organization. They're more passionate about the business than anyone in headquarters would ever believe possible. And they are so knowledgeable and sophisticated about the methods for greater productivity. A boss has to be thinking, 'If I had just 20 percent of my people talking and working like these folks, my problems would be over.'

"Typically, in the beginning some of the team members are really concerned about making presentations. They say, 'I don't like making speeches. I don't know how.'" But Sharma tells them, "Don't worry. Just speak from the heart."

Because of this presentation, all the company's CAVE people are totally outmaneuvered.

Turf wars are history, senior VPs taking credit for a subordinate's contribution is over, executive excuses like saying "What can we do? We've got a union" won't cut it anymore. The top boss has seen undeniable proof that there is immense power to improve the business using the people who already work for the company.

"The CEO has seen the energy, the passion, the intelligence, and the potential of the workforce that is turned on at work," Sharma said. He can calculate the guaranteed increases in productivity and the better returns on investment. All he has to do is harness the energy and blow out the bureaucracy. No CEO will leave that session allowing any CAVE person to get in the way of the necessary changes taking hold.

"You see," said Sharma, "you *can* teach an old dog new tricks." All you have to do is get past the CAVE people.

8 GET EVERYONE TO "JUST LET GO"

■

Anything new is going to encounter opposition. It's the way it has always been. Every organization has an immune system with antibodies that attack all changes automatically.

In the last chapter, Anand Sharma of TBM Consulting labeled these antibodies the "citizens against virtually everything" (CAVE people). Sharma provided four tactics to outmaneuver your company's CAVE people and win the battle for more buy-in. But winning one battle is only the beginning for managers concerned with following through.

You see, there's a CAVE person inside each of us. We all have a tendency to hold on to our old ideas and worn-out ways, stubbornly refusing to change. That means every company is filled with potential obstructers ready to get in the way of the organization's follow-through. Managers need to do more than outmaneuver the opponents to any *single* new idea. They need to show everyone on their team how to instinctively let go of this impulsive reaction, of attacking anything new and unfamiliar.

That's the lesson that can be learned through the story of one of Sharma's first clients, an eighty-year-old manufacturing company from Pella, Iowa.

A COMPANY WITHOUT CAVE PEOPLE

If Hollywood were going to tell the world a story of the ideal modern organization—where thousands of employees and managers enthusiastically drop their set ways and readily follow through on a change in direction—they probably wouldn't select an eighty-year-old window and door maker from Pella, Iowa. Pella is a small, conservative city in the Midwest, founded by a nineteenth-century minister who left Holland because the state-run Dutch church wasn't *strict enough.*

But Pella, Iowa, is home to the Pella Corporation, a world-class manufacturer of premium-quality windows, entry-door systems, storm doors, and patio doors. Pella is also a world-class example of a couple of the most productive new concepts in business: lean manufacturing and continuous process improvement. As you've no doubt gleaned from their previous mentions in this book, lean manufacturing and continuous process improvement mean constant change for employees and managers. Whatever someone's doing and however they're doing it at a "lean" company, it's going to change, sooner rather than later.

Ten to twelve times a week, fifty-two weeks a year, staffers, production workers, and managers from across Pella's many manufacturing plants and central offices "kaizen" some long-standing manufacturing method or entrenched company process. (Reminder: *kaizen* is a Japanese word meaning "to take apart and put back together in a better way.") So far, more than 29,000 team members (employees, managers, and outside associates) have participated in these kaizen events.

By taking the company's manufacturing and management processes apart and putting them back together in a better way almost 5,000 times over ten years, Pella has transformed their business. According to J. Cunningham and O. Fiume, the authors of the book *Real Numbers: Management Accounting in a Lean Organization,* Pella's lead times have been reduced by 65 percent, sales have more than doubled, and profits are up six times. Equally important is the fact that Pella has achieved these ends while being rated the twelfth-best place in America to work by *Fortune* magazine, ahead of Microsoft, Cisco, and Intel.

As impressive as the company's results are, what should grab your attention the most is the fact that, unlike most companies, Pella can take apart any business process—from the shop floor, from the administrative functions, and even from headquarters—and make it more productive without any bureaucratic interference or stubborn obstruction from an old-school manager or employee. How? People at Pella don't obstruct changes, they embrace them. They've transformed themselves from CAVE people into more modern men and women, creating a company willing to let go and follow through on new ideas enthusiastically.

HOW PELLA LEARNED TO LET GO

Mel Haught (now the CEO of Pella Corporation) was the vice president of manufacturing in 1993 when he participated in the first kaizen event at Pella. Haught saw right away that the biggest challenge of turning that onetime success into a long-term competitive advantage wouldn't be taking work processes apart, brainstorming significant improvements, or even getting more buy-in for the proposed changes. The biggest challenge would be keeping everyone from holding on to old ideas and worn-out ways. "We found we had to let go," Haught said.

Haught decided to lead this change in attitude by example:

First, he says, "I had to let go of the notion that the boss had to be the smartest person in the room."

When the boss believes he or she has to be seen as the smartest person in the room, they are likely to, in Haught's words, "hijack the dialog." This shows up in the way they run a meeting. Managers worried about being the smartest come to a discussion with a firm idea of what the outcome should be. They subtly (and not so subtly) let participants know what it is they should be saying and thinking—checking their watch when subordinates are speaking, showing they're irritated when they see someone take the conversation off topic, and generally making comments that tell subordinates, "Don't go there."

Haught learned that if executives let go of their egos and stop hijacking the dialog, they will discover that extremely valuable input can come from every level of their company.

At Pella, kaizen teams are cross-functional and cut diagonally across the hierarchy. They have groups that include executives and hourly workers, people who are part of the process at hand and those who've never set foot in the plant. According to Haught, doing it this way has been a real eye-opener. "Listening to people who have no direct experience in the specific process we're targeting for enhancement really helped our improvement process. They [people without experience] ask some of those good *dumb* questions like, 'Why do we do it that way?' that really clear away the hidden assumptions."

Listening to "dumb" questions and being asked to reconsider their assumptions would irritate many executives, but not Haught. "Hourly people had some of the best input," he said. All he had to do was to let go of the idea that the boss (or consultant or professor) had to be the smartest one there.

And as Haught was seen letting go of his ego, the rest of the company let go of theirs.

Second, he says, "I had to let go [of perfectionism]."

We all want perfect answers. Going back to a subject again and again seems like a waste of time. The CAVE person knows this and will throw up a lot of "what ifs," hoping to convince a team not to try something until they have studied a solution (to death).

CAVE people know that constantly asking "what if" can intimidate others into keeping their mouths shut. The hidden message in a "what if" question is "You'd better have a perfect answer or you'll be embarrassed." It's designed to kill fresh ideas and out-of-the-box input during group discussions.

Here's how it works: A participant will offer an idea and a CAVE person will propose a scenario and ask a question like "How would your solution fit this *what if* situation?" When the participant can't answer the hypothetical convincingly, they feel as if they should keep their ideas to themselves until they've considered every potential problem (which can take forever). CAVE people use this tactic to stop everyone from suggesting change.

Letting go of such perfectionism has made change a lot easier to suggest at Pella. "It's much *less* acceptable now [at Pella] to do nothing," Haught explained, "than to do something and have to go back later and make additional changes."

Which led Haught to let go of another old idea.

"I had to let go of my ideas about failure," he said.

When somebody asked Haught, "Have you ever had a kaizen event not achieve its full potential?" he knew what they meant. Part of the perfectionist attitude is the concept that one small failure disqualifies any new idea. So CAVE people look for an example where the change didn't work instead of the tens (or hundreds) of times it did work.

CAVE people refuse to recognize that the glass might be half full. When Haught was asked if he'd ever had a failure, he redefined the word to make a point about letting go. "Have we ever had a kaizen that didn't achieve all we intended? Sure," Haught answered. "But that isn't how I define failure anymore."

Haught asks instead, "Have we ever had a kaizen event that didn't achieve substantial progress?" His answer? "Absolutely not."

"You have to let go [of a narrow definition of success]," Haught concluded. And by letting go of this narrow definition, Haught said, "We've learned it was still very productive even when we had to go back to the same process *five or six times*."

Through Haught's willingness to lead by example and a decade of following through on the principles of kaizen, Pella has become a company without CAVE people. They let go of their old processes and worn-out ways without hesitation.

What if your company doesn't practice the kaizen disciplines, or if your top executives won't let go themselves? Is there another way a team can change its CAVE-person tendencies into an instinctive willingness to let go?

From an assignment last year, I learned one very successful way to help staff make the transition from CAVE people to mature, open men and women.

In the fall of 2003, a renowned Fortune 50 organization called me for help. They needed fresh ideas for growth; conditions outside of the company were changing faster than the people on the inside. I knew their industry and their customers well. I had lots of ideas to share with them.

Then I remembered John Maynard Keynes's famous words: "The difficulty lies not so much in developing new ideas as in escaping from old ones." So instead of brainstorming ideas for revenue growth with this client, I followed these three steps to teach their people to let go:

1. I opened a dialogue with executives about some examples of companies and industries that held on when they should have let go.
2. I told them a story of the Malay monkey trap.
3. I asked them to list the things they would like to let go of.

Then I asked them to break into teams of twelve participants and imagine what they'd do to generate more growth. After an hour, each group gave the senior managers their conclusions. The executives heard enough new *good* ideas to declare my mission accomplished.

I hadn't given them a single one of *my* new ideas. All they got from me was a discussion about letting go. That was all it took.

Here is a complete syllabus for that meeting. I offer it as a template for your own session to help your people let go of the CAVE person mind-set and turn into a staff that can buy in to new ideas and follow through unhesitatingly.

TEACHING YOUR TEAM TO "LET GO": START WITH A DIALOGUE

Start a conversation with your people on the negative effects of holding on to old ideas, worn-out products and services, and other CAVE-person tendencies. Here are three good examples for such a discussion:

1. How did Dell move from operating out of a dorm room in 1985 to becoming the number-one PC-market-share leader in the world? They didn't invent a faster processor or new hard drive. Dell implemented a strategy of just-in-time manufacturing and sales direct to the consumer—rather than through

retail outlets—that saved customers money. But for years before they became an overwhelming force in the industry, the company's strategy was apparent to every competitor and could have been copied at any time. Why didn't Compaq, IBM, Apple, or any other major computer maker reexamine their business model and figure out how, by duplicating Dell's strategy, they could save customers money and improve their own competitive position? *Because Dell's competitors couldn't let go of their old ways of manufacturing and distribution.*

2. Remember the ad "It's not your father's Oldsmobile?" GM spent hundreds of millions trying to breathe life into that historic brand. But America had long before decided the car wasn't their father's Oldsmobile . . . it was Grandpa's. The name was dead for years before GM pulled the plug. Meanwhile, other GM brands were starved for the cash they needed to build their businesses. Why did the brightest managers with access to the most intelligent consultants and market research throw so much good money into a failing product line? *Because GM's decision makers couldn't let go of yesterday's breadwinner.*

3. *Encyclopaedia Britannica* was once a gem of the publishing business. They had a product with a unit cost of $250 that sold for $1,500. In 1990, the company did $650 million at those attractive margins. But over the next few years, more than half of their buyers disappeared, selecting a far inferior CD-ROM version that came bundled with a new computer. Britannica had to have known this could happen. Their research showed that people were sold not on the 65,000 articles and 24,000 photos, graphs, illustrations, and charts that was the *Encyclopaedia Britannica,* but on the idea they were investing in "something good for the kids." Why didn't Britannica realize that something good for the kids in the 1990s had become a computer, and put together their own digital version of their encyclopedia (bundled with their own computer) and keep their customers? *Because Britannica's salespeople wouldn't*

let go of their $500-per-unit commission, and management
wouldn't let go of them.

Each of these situations describes a company or an industry unable
to move when they should have, owing to the fact that they couldn't
let go. These were not rational decisions. People were trapped by a
primitive instinct invisible to managers and to organizations.

As we've already covered, you're not going to reason somebody
out of something they didn't reason themselves into. The best way
to get people to stop holding on irrationally is to present this irrational urge in its proper perspective—as a dangerous impulse we
share with our cousin (the monkey) on the evolutionary scale.

TRAPPED BY THEIR INSTINCTS INSTEAD OF A NET

On a small island off the coast of Singapore, there was a four-star resort
with a new championship golf course. Designed by an internationally
famous celebrity golfer, the course featured panoramic vistas and gor-
geous landscaping. The front nine overlooked the South China Sea,
while the back nine was bordered by the lush Indonesian rainforest.

Shortly after the course opened, a troop of silver-leaf monkeys
came to nest in the mangroves off the fifteenth hole. The creatures
weren't dangerous. They only came down from the trees occasion-
ally to snatch a ball or ransack an unattended golf cart. But management saw the potential for more serious problems and decided
to rid the course of these cute little pests.

They hired an expert who suggested drawing the monkeys out of
the trees with food. As they devoured the treats, he explained, his
people could drop a net over them. Then they could cage the troop
and relocate them to the far side of the island.

But when the expert was asked if this was a safe process, in line
with humane treatment, he explained that most attempts to trap
monkeys resulted in a 50 percent mortality rate. "Everyone knows,"
the expert said, "monkeys are too high-strung to all survive capture."

One of the resort's Malaysian managers offered another idea.
His grandfather used something called a "Malay monkey trap" to

remove monkeys from the gardens in his village. "Grandfather said the Malay monkey trap always captures a monkey alive," he told his peers. Then he explained how it worked.

"Grandfather would collect several heavy ceramic jars with very narrow necks and place them where the monkeys could see the jars," the manager explained. "Then he'd drop some fragrant fruits and delicious nuts to the bottom of each. The trap was then baited and grandfather would retreat out of sight.

"Before long, the curious monkeys would drop down from the trees to see what my grandfather left behind. Smelling the aroma of some favorite foods, the monkeys would each thrust an arm deep to the bottom of each jar and grab a fistful."

The trap was then sprung. The creatures' fists, filled with nuts and fruit pieces, were now too big to fit back through the narrow necks of the jars. Each monkey was handcuffed, unable to move as the jar was too heavy to budge. After a few minutes of fussing and crying, the primates would become docile. "Then," the Malaysian manager finished his story, "grandfather would gently cage each animal."

"I don't understand," said one of the other managers. "Why doesn't the monkey just drop the nuts and break free?"

"Instinct," the Malaysian manager replied. "Once a monkey has something it likes in its grasp, the animal can't let it go."

TEAM EXERCISE: THE FOUR COMMON MONKEY TRAPS FOR MANAGERS

Instead of fruits and nuts, managers and organizations get trapped by blinders, comfort zones, sacred cows, and sunk costs. Ask them to list examples of each category at your company.

1. Blinders

Every businessperson has beliefs about business, products, and people. As they put their beliefs to the test, they discover where they were right, where they were wrong, and adapt. But after a string of successes, this cycle stops. Beliefs become dogma, and rather than seeing where their beliefs are no longer valid, managers put on a set of blinders.

AOL is a perfect example of this. So many of the disabling facts that came to light after the Time Warner merger in 2000 were known a year or more before it all hit the fan. For example, ad managers couldn't get the message through to the top brass that "a lot of their advertisers will be nonrecurring" (they wouldn't be renewing their multimillion-dollar commitments for sponsorships and advertising). AOL's top execs closed their eyes and ears and nobody did anything to fix the problem. This cost the company plenty. Its ad revenue went from $2.3 billion in 2001 down to $1.3 billion in 2002 and slid another 35 to 45 percent in 2003, according to the *Wall Street Journal*.

Kodak offers another good corporate example.

Innovation, hard work, and good luck had made Kodak a monolith in the photographic industry. In 1981, the Rochester, New York–based manufacturer sold nine out of every ten rolls of film bought in the United States and Canada.

But as the eighties ended, "[executives] who had been successful doing things one way [were unable] to even consider doing things another way," according to Bill Zollars, who spent twenty-plus years in the hierarchy at the company. (Zollars is now the head of Yellow Roadway Corporation.)

These blinders concerned Zollars. He knew that any company with a 90 percent market share had only one way to go, and that was down.

Zollars told his friend George Fisher (the new CEO), "Don't underestimate the power of the culture at this company, because it is an *unbelievable* immovable force." But Fisher didn't realize how strong it was.

Three years later, Fisher told Zollars that he "did [indeed] underestimate it." As *BusinessWeek* reported in October of '97, "[Fisher] hasn't been able to change the huge mass of middle managers." By 2000, Fisher had left but the blinders stayed.

In 2004, the company revealed that they (again) had not seen how fast consumers would change to filmless (digital) cameras. Kodak announced another round of still-deeper layoffs and cut their stock dividend 72 percent. As of the summer of 2004, their stock price was stuck near where it was back in 1982, and Kodak is no longer one of the companies used to compute the Dow Jones Industrial Average.

2. Comfort Zones

Every business is filled with worn-out ways of doing things. They could all benefit from reinventing their processes. But in general, that doesn't happen. Most organizations have an irrational urge to stay in their comfort zones.

Look at what one executive at a large retail company had to go through to change one small report for the better:

"My people had trouble finding the answers we needed in one of our weekly summaries," the exec, a vice president and divisional manager, explained. "So an associate took a similar report from another division and altered it [to fit their department's needs] with the hope it would give us the data we needed." Later, when she printed the new format, she discovered that it had completely solved the problem. The new template spread through the division, and within two weeks everybody was using it. "We were all pretty excited. All the numbers we needed were now at our fingertips," Anne (not her real name) said.

But the excitement was short-lived. Anne's group shared the report with one other department, and unfortunately *their* VP refused to let go of her old ways. "You need to use the original format when you submit your numbers to us," she told Anne immediately after receiving the altered report. "What you just sent me doesn't give us enough information."

Anne was irritated.

You see, Anne is in an industry that has been slow to change over the last twenty years and it has cost them dearly. New entrants have taken market share away from her company and others who once led their industry—simply because the new companies were quicker to innovate. In response, her company's leadership has made it a top priority since 1998 for the organization to become more creative, innovative, and challenging. Here are quotes from several letters to shareholders in their annual reports: (1998) "To remain a leader we must continually adapt and change with the times"; (1999) "Strive to reinvent"; (2000) "Take prudent risks rather than do nothing"; (2001) "Standing still gets you nowhere"; and (2002) "Seek and pursue new ideas."

Anne had worked hard to follow through on these expectations. She changed her team's attitude about adapting quickly and has encouraged them to seek every opportunity to become more productive.

So while Anne was happy to have a better report format, she was downright thrilled that her people had taken the initiative to reinvent a process for the better. Now her counterpart's stubbornness threatened to send everyone on her team the wrong signal.

Anne decided to talk it over and try to reason with the other VP. "Maybe I introduced the new format too abruptly," Anne thought. "If I show her our thinking and explain how this supports the larger corporate goal . . . she'll change her mind."

She started by listening to her counterpart's criticism that some data was lost in the new format. "But the extra information from the old format is unnecessary most of the time," Anne explained. "I think the speed and accuracy this new format adds to our weekly decision making outweighs the occasional need for a bit more detail." She concluded, "And your own people seem to agree. Your secretary just came to me and said, 'Hey, the report your group uses is better than the one we've been using.' She wants a copy for your people!"

But this old-school supervisor wasn't about to let go of her comfort zone. "The report was better the way it was," she told Anne, ending the discussion and dismissing Anne.

So now, every week, Anne's assistant spends hours putting the summary back into the old format for no one but this old-school manager. And everyone got the not-so-subtle message: *Think twice before you start changing anything for the better. It will be more trouble than it's worth.*

3. Sacred Cows

Carolyn was the chief accountant in an electronics company. She was a typical old-school controller, usually upset about some missing piece of paperwork or a customer request that was not part of the routine. What was not typical was her disregard for everyone outside the world of accounting. She treated sales managers like a bother and obstructed any request that wasn't done according to the process manual. But when a top executive was told that she was an obstruction in the way of his goal to double revenues, the president replied, "Figure something out . . . she's staying." You see, Carolyn had been around for twenty years and had become a sacred cow in his organization.

After Bill Zollars left Kodak, he was hired to turn around the losses at Yellow Transportation. Zollars knew things had to change at Yellow. In his mind, that change would start with clearing out all the sacred cows at headquarters.

Zollars chose ten executives to help him sort through all the brass in the home office. "Okay," he told them, "we're going to build teams. It's going to be like the NFL draft. Tell me who you want and we'll balance these teams out." The first name that came up was a HR guy who had been around for twenty years.

Zollars told the group they were going to cull through the sacred cows. "Jack, you're the first one up," he announced. "If you can't give me a solid reason you shouldn't have this guy on your team in about two sentences, he's yours!" That's all it took. The floodgates opened and Jack was adamant: "I don't want him," he claimed, noting the HR guy's ineffectiveness.

Then the next guy came up and again Zollars saw people looking at their shoes. "Ted?" he called out. Ted knew what was coming and spoke up immediately: "I don't want him." Then Ted explained what was wrong and how the guy didn't fit in.

Soon everybody was identifying the sacred cows among the headquarters staff.

"We had a breakthrough," Zollars remembered. "Everybody saw this was real life-and-death stuff. We weren't going to play games. We had to get the right people on the bus and get the other people out." And so by letting go of sacred cows, Yellow Transportation jump-started their transformation.

Sacred cows exist among staff, customers, and even suppliers. To decide who they are, ask yourself, "Who wouldn't cut it if we were starting out fresh?" The list will tell you if you are holding on when you should be letting go.

4. Sunk Costs

"Sunk costs" is a concept from negotiation strategy.

It describes the situation where a businessperson is willingly trapped into taking a bad deal because he can't let go of his ego. Some people would say sunk costs are where executives throw good money after bad.

It works like this: Imagine a contractor goes out to estimate a new job. He spends a couple of hours asking and answering questions, taking measurements, writing a proposal, and spends a week following up on the phone—all without closing the deal. Now he knows it is bad business to invest any more effort without a commitment from the customer. But then he spends another week answering new questions, estimating four other options, delivering a couple of additional proposals, all the while telling his people about the new job he's about to land. If after all that time and effort the client finally offers him less than it costs to do the job, he is tempted to take the bad deal. "After all," he thinks, "I don't want to waste all the work I've put into this job." All that work is a sunk cost. He can't recover it. All he can do is save face.

European banks spent a fortune building up large equities operations to compete with global investment bankers like Goldman Sachs, Merrill Lynch, and Morgan Stanley. According to Charles Roxburgh of McKinsey's London Office, "It proved extraordinarily hard for some of these banks to face up to the strategic reality that they had no prospect of ever competing successfully."

Why? Roxburgh says the reason is loss aversion. "We would rather spend an additional $10 million completing an uneconomic $110-million project than write off $100 million." Of course, Roxburgh knows that sometime soon the entire $110 million will be taken as a loss. In other words, it will be sunk costs.

A handful of sunk costs can trap even the most sophisticated business executives.

When a CEO assigns her best people to fix a troubled project because she personally approved the original bad idea, or when an executive insists the sales staff continue to sell to his old customers even though they cost more to service than they spend, or when the president refuses to abandon a onetime major breadwinning product that's been going backward for years . . . they are all trapped with their fists full of sunk costs.

The only way out of these traps is to learn to let go.

9 CREATE A HOT TEAM

Y ou know what a HOT team is, don't you? You've probably
been on one at least once in your life. Maybe you didn't think
of it as a HOT team, or maybe you've just forgotten. Here's a short
story to jog your memory:

It was 1972 and I needed money for college. So I got a job as a
janitor and was assigned to work the day shift at a start-up technology company in Mountain View, California.

One day, the plant's general manager asked to see me. "The fore-
men, engineers, and production people all like you," he said. "We're
looking for young people to join us. How would you like to become
one of our engineering technicians?"

Within a week, I was hired. This was the first really serious job I
ever had. In the past, I had only pumped gas or swept floors. Now I
was mixing dangerous acids for etching silicon wafers, hooking up
noxious gases to make layers of microscopic circuits, and checking
the ultra-high temperature of industrial ovens prior to baking the
MOS (metal-oxide-silicon) discs. Once I poured two things that
shouldn't have been mixed together down a drain. The gas that
came up from that mistake sent me to the emergency room.

But it isn't the technical knowledge or hazards that I remember most. What really stands out in my memory is how energized I felt every day I showed up for work at that company—a level of buy-in that I've tried to duplicate in every job since.

The day-to-day mood in the plant was incredible. It was an assembly line–style workplace, with different rooms of people doing the same things over and over. But nobody ever seemed to be bored. Everyone was really interested in their jobs and in one another. They all talked about their work—quality control, breakage percentages, and how the company was doing in general—as well as the typical personal topics at lunch, on breaks, even after hours at the local beer garden.

Sometimes on Fridays the executives put on aprons and spent the afternoon cooking hamburgers and hot dogs at a company party. In the summertime, there were evening softball games and everybody showed up. We regularly ate lunch in big groups. Senior executives, people with advanced technical degrees, and the blue-collar staff all mixed easily. And although the work was demanding and challenges came up daily, I never watched the clock or failed to give an assignment every ounce of my effort. I even went to the library to check out books about the chemical and electrical engineering principles used at the plant so I could understand more about what we were doing.

One day, a supervising engineer (not my boss) pulled me aside after he overheard some sarcastic remark I had made about one of the front-line workers. He said, "Hey, everybody here makes an important contribution. And they have to be good or they wouldn't be here. I know you aren't serious, but don't let anyone hear you talk like that." I was surprised. Here was a boss, not mine and not the boss of the production line, looking out for the feelings of one of the front-line, hourly employees. And he had enough interest in me to *coach* me on showing respect and valuing every member of the team rather than just yelling at me.

When I had enough money for my first year of college, I told my supervisor I was sorry but that I had to leave. The manager and his boss both asked me to stay (they had a tuition assistance program they wanted me to try), or at least come back after I graduated. I replied, "Thanks, but no thanks. I have other plans."

At the time, I thought this was what *every* modern organization would be like—friendly and open with incredible esprit de corps, a meritocracy where Ph.D.s and front-line workers all got along, where people worked hard but enjoyed it, where there was always something fun to look forward to.

Boy, was I wrong. I didn't realize it at the time, but I had accidentally happened upon one of the greatest HOT teams in business history. Soon after I left, that small company got really successful and became a rock star in the technology world. But in 1972, Intel was an unknown.

HOT teams are where work is fun and, when the day ends, you can't wait for tomorrow. HOT teams are where everyone gets a lot done in less time without anyone barking orders or breathing down the team's collective neck.

Hard work doesn't feel nearly as draining on a HOT team as it does elsewhere, and sacrifices are typically no big deal. Problems get solved without a lot of fuss, although not because everybody on the team always agrees. If there is a rift, a HOT team discusses it like adults and pulls together again quickly.

The genius of HOT teams is it doesn't matter who's on the team—strong-willed individualists, soft-hearted coordinators, creative types, bean counters, old hands, and new hires. HOT teams have a way of getting everyone in even the most diverse groups to do their level best to follow through.

That's because morale is great on a HOT team. And that great morale creates an environment where the law of inertia doesn't have as much pull and buy-in is easier to get and sustain.

So now that I've jogged your memory, the big question is "Do you know how to make your own team a HOT team?"

A COOL MANAGER CREATES HOT TEAMS

When manufacturers have a huge challenge in front of them—when there's a significant opportunity and they need the utmost in creative thinking and fast action—they call IDEO, the Silicon Valley–based design firm.

IDEO has provided the creative genius behind more than 3,000 special projects and innovations. The company has had a hand in everyday things like Apple's mouse, the Palm V personal desktop assistant, Nike's V-12 sunglasses, and Oral B's children's toothbrushes. They've also handled more exotic projects, like a video-equipped miniature submarine, a defibrillator so easy to use a six-year-old can save a life, and a one-person pedal-powered water pump for irrigating parched crops in underdeveloped countries.

But one of this innovative company's most impressive creations is their in-house approach to great workplace morale. IDEO has discovered how to make a team HOT on demand.

Tom Kelley, one of the managers of IDEO, is a very cool guy. Tall and friendly, he is calm, approachable, and has a razor-sharp mind. He's as ready to listen as he is to talk, which makes him an easy guy to learn from.

What Kelley knows about creating HOT teams doesn't come from workshops or university courses. "Our learning came from being in the trenches," he said. "That kind of 'Hey that worked . . . Boy that was stupid . . . Yikes let's never do that again' knowledge you only get when you're busy *doing*. Most experts go from the general to the specific. Our understanding of HOT teams comes from the other direction. We didn't systematically toy with the variables. We just built a prototype. If something worked, we noticed it and stuck with it."

That practical wisdom has led to insights into HOT teams that any manager can easily use. Kelley described his prototype with a list of dos and don'ts:

THE DON'TS OF HOT TEAMS

DON'T BECOME RULE-BOUND.

Organizations tend to take the need for rational boundaries and intelligent controls to absurd lengths. As a result they become rule-bound, making being at work more irritating and demotivating.

"I have a friend," Kelley said, "and she went to work for a law firm.

One day she came in and pinned up a poster. It was a nice poster . . . a piece of art. Within an hour, someone came and took it down." The woman was told she had broken the rules. "First of all, *we* do not use pushpins here," the office manager said with a condescending smile, "and second, all art must be approved by the *art* committee."

As any thinking manager should see, such an exchange is horrible for morale. By removing that woman's poster and admonishing her as if she were a misbehaving child, the company sent their new hire a chilling message:

- We don't trust your judgment.
- We don't respect your feelings.
- We're watching you.

Kelley believes that it isn't only the over-the-top, bureaucratic rules that are bad for HOT teams. In his mind, every impulse to create a rule must be carefully scrutinized.

Imagine this much less extreme situation: A well intentioned leader, anxious to save time in a brainstorming session, creates a rule that says, "We want all the good ideas in the world . . . but only if they're *manufacturable*."

Or picture this: An equally well-intentioned leader, anxious to make sure everyone has a chance to talk in a meeting, makes this rule: "We'll go around the table and everyone will have two minutes to talk."

The manufacturable idea rule is intended to eliminate wasting time on impractical concepts. The two-minute rule is intended to keep a few personalities from dominating the discussion and to increase participation. But by using these rules, the managers have come up with a cure that is worse than the disease.

The problem with the first rule, according to Kelley, is that it limits everyone's ability to have an open mind. "That [rule about only wanting ideas that are manufacturable] starts everybody editing themselves before they speak," Kelley said. "'Oh, here's a thought,' they would think. 'No, wait, that can't be done.' Or, 'Oh, I'd like to suggest . . . No, we've tried that before.'"

The rule about having two minutes to talk is just as restrictive,

Kelley said. "I remember there was a meeting at a client's offices. Sixteen of us were seated around a big table and we were told we should take turns talking. It felt more like a student council meeting," Kelley explained, "than a creative session."

If your goal is a HOT team brainstorming session, it would be better to let things start out messy and clean them up later. And if your goal is to encourage more participation on your HOT team, learn how to draw out the quieter personalities, or keep the overbearing personalities out of your meeting or on a leash, rather than using an egg-timer approach that makes the group even more bureaucratic.

Becoming rule-bound like this is the unintended result of a useful and valuable business practice called *process*.

Process is all about standardizing tasks—highlighting inefficiencies and inconsistencies to reduce defects and increase reliability and repeatability. Process helps organizations control the workplace. But when you take the principles of process too far, you get a *process police state* like the one Kelley's friend worked at, with an art committee and local spies who report on rule breakers to the authorities.

Supporting an uptight and overly structured environment is clearly toxic to HOT teams. Avoid it at all costs.

DON'T BE UNFAIR.

The need to keep teams HOT at AOL was dealt a body blow by the way employees known as "FOBs" (Friends of COO Bob Pittman) were treated. These people with political connections to one of AOL's top executives were often the least competent associates in their units. But they were never singled out during the group's performance reviews. And when the company was forced to lay off hundreds of employees, the FOBs were protected. The result? Everyone realized that the performance-management system at AOL was unfair.

Unfairness also afflicted the HOT teams at a major telecom company.

The company implemented a GE-style ranking system, where employees are graded every year and the weakest links are weeded out. But according to insiders, a significant number of employees and midlevel managers figured out how to "game" the evaluation system and prevent a fair comparison.

"I have some people I want to protect, so I now hire some people I know will be low performers," one manager admitted. By adding someone he knows will underperform the group, the manager creates a group of sacrificial lambs. "When it's time to get rid of someone, I've got someone to throw to the wolves."

Some employees at that same company make a big show of being good teammates, while hoarding their best ideas and sabotaging others when management isn't watching.

"Even though teamwork and cooperation are part of the objectives, they don't matter as much as accomplishing your goals," the insider explained. So by hoarding their knowledge and undermining others who are trying to be good teammates, these schemers make sure there's always someone below them in the rankings.

"Plus," the insider revealed, "managers skew the rankings with their personal opinions. It's all about how your manager feels about you and how upper management feels about your manager. It's very demoralizing."

HOT teams are about having a *"peer-oriented* meritocracy," Kelley explained. A meritocracy is a system where people compete and succeed based on their actual performance, instead of on their political skills or contacts. Peer-oriented meritocracy means that evaluations come mostly from team members, not the team leaders. Kelley believes it's the fairest way to decide who should and shouldn't be rewarded.

"A general manager might come by one hour a week," Kelley said, "and look around to see who looks like they're doing stuff. If you put too much reliance on the boss's impressions in judging the group, we think that opens the door for that 'Eddie Haskell' kind of individual who can fool the boss one hour a week but can't fool the team members the other thirty-nine hours a week." (Eddie

Haskell, a fifties/sixties character on the sitcom *Leave It to Beaver*, was incredibly polite and proper in front of authority figures and a weasel and cheat behind their backs.)

"Our performance appraisals are done by peers," Kelley explained, stressing that they are the most reliable sources for knowing who's meeting expectations and who's letting the team down. "The boss is in the room, because in the end the boss has to make some decisions," Kelley said. "But the data comes directly from the peers."

Unfairness is corrosive to the mind-set of HOT teams. It dissolves trust and leaves people resentful, itching for payback.

DON'T BE MEAN.

Facing changing conditions, tough competition, demands for higher returns, and intense time pressures, many executives feel they have no choice but to take a hard line. "We need to become lean and mean," they'll announce.

They are half right. Lean is a business necessity.

But mean adds no value to HOT teams whatsoever. All mean tactics do is make organizations more rigid, keep executives from seeing problems before they become disasters, prompt bad judgment and unethical practices, and leave HOT teams cold.

Take Richard Brown's tenure at Electronic Data Systems as a case in point.

When Richard Brown took over Electronic Data Systems in early 1999, the company had been mired in years of flat revenues with no growth in market share and declining earnings. Brown analyzed the shortfall. He decided the problems were internal and that they needed a culture change to become lean and mean.

Brown set goals for immediate revenue and sales growth that most people in the company thought would be impossible to meet and instituted practices to hold everybody's feet to the fire:

• He gathered his 150 top executives on a conference call every month and singled out anyone who missed budget to answer tough questions in public. "He'd ask you why in front of everyone," a former executive told the *Wall Street Journal*. And Brown expected the manager to tell the group on the spot what precisely was going to be done to get back on budget.

- He made it clear that poor performers should shape up or leave. When he discovered 20 percent of the sales staff had sold nothing in the preceding six months, he asked executives, "What are you going to do about these people and their supervisors?" They knew what he wanted. The 20 percent were quickly replaced.

- When an executive told Brown he was worried about anxiety and unrest in his business unit caused by the massive reorganization and stretch goals, Brown jumped all over him. "This is a test of leadership. You show me an organization that's wringing its hands, listening to rumors, anxious about the future, and I will show you leadership that behaves the same way. People imitate their leaders. I can't believe this worry is fact-based. I believe their worry is ignorance-based. And if that's the case, it's your fault."*

Brown's combination of lean with mean apparently worked for a while. In his first thirty-five months, EDS signed more new business ($88.9 billion) than they'd signed in the previous thirteen years. And every other metric at the company went way up as well—EDS had eleven consecutive quarters of double-digit growth in operating margins and earnings per share.

But in the fifteen months that followed, things took a decided turn for the worse.

- New megaclients like WorldCom and US Air went bankrupt and other high-profile new contracts were renegotiated downward.

- Cash flow dropped significantly and EDS had to tell Wall Street their earnings projections would be off by 80 percent.

- EDS paid a $3.7-million fine to settle charges of double-billing a Medicaid contract.

- Serious questions were raised about EDS's accounting practices, according to the *Wall Street Journal*.

*L. Bossidy and R. Charan, *Execution*, Crown Business, 2002.

- The company's stock crashed, falling 71 percent from its highs in 2001 and 60 percent from what it was when Brown arrived.
- And Brown was asked to resign.
  What happened?
  All the predictable outcomes of connecting mean with lean.
- Most managers would do almost anything to avoid having to say in front of 150 of their peers, "I screwed up."
- Because people who aired their concerns about EDS's strategy were treated like "hand-wringers" and had their commitment questioned, employees learned to keep quiet about other problems in the making.
- As employees saw people fired for not bringing in enough new deals, or hitting an impossible budget, they learned to say and do anything to sell somebody a deal and hit their plan.

Mean managers say they're merely being tough-minded and results-oriented. But beneath their demands for high standards and dealing with problems in a firm and consistent way is a callous disregard for people's feelings and the effect on employee morale. Mean tactics humiliate, scapegoat, and manipulate. They create bullies who attack people instead of problems and make everyone feel the organization doesn't care. They will ruin your HOT teams. Run from them.

Here's a suggestion for other practices to avoid. Take a look at one of the compilations of *Dilbert* comic strips by Scott Adams. In essence, Adams has chronicled virtually all the don'ts for HOT teams. In Dilbert's world, everybody feels as if "I have to do what I'm doing because my *stupid* boss came up with this *stupid* idea. . . ." Everybody is made to feel smaller, less competent, defeated, and angry by attacks on their self-esteem, arbitrary slights, and unwarranted impositions. It's a toxic environment where staff capabilities shrivel and the sum of the parts becomes *less* than the whole.

You don't need a workshop in organizational psychology to decide what things you shouldn't do—just read *Dilbert* and steer clear of anything (and everything) that makes Dilbert's world cubicle hell.

THE DOS OF HOT TEAMS

There are as many ways to build great morale as there are organizations. But there are some particular themes that help to turn a regular workgroup into a HOT team. These themes are the five dos:

1. Like your people.
2. Believe in them.
3. Listen to them.
4. Make teamwork engaging.
5. Let them decide.

LIKE YOUR PEOPLE.

Dr. Harry Levinson teaches that a manager's feelings toward her staff will make or break the morale of a team. "What's so special about the place . . . where you find a whole group of people who obviously enjoy working together day after day?" Levinson asks in his publication *The Levinson Letter*. "A big part is the manager. She *likes* all her people."

Mark Kuroczko is an example of Levinson's observation—a boss who created a HOT team simply by liking his people.

Kuroczko was in charge of a small department responsible for writing technical manuals and spec sheets for a big banking organization. Since these were low-profile projects with a lot of dreary details and little glamour, Kuroczko didn't have to answer to the chief of marketing communications.

So instead of more corporate people with communications degrees and years in the financial business, Kuroczko hired painters, musicians, novelists, and even a sculptor—creative types that he liked to be around. Because he liked them, he was especially protective. "I saw my job as manager to create a game preserve for creative beasts," he said. "I wanted to protect our little group of fun people, doing fun projects safe from the corporate types and bureaucratic interference."

But every move Kuroczko made to protect his band of "creative beasts" from the bureaucracy had the unexpected effect of showing each person how much Kuroczko liked them. In return, they showed Kuroczko something he never would have anticipated.

One day an executive VP couldn't get the support he needed from the bank's main marketing and communications department. So he called Kuroczko and asked if he could take charge and do a critical four-color brochure and some associated client proposals. Kuroczko said sure.

When his team got hold of the project, they were unbelievably responsive and inventive. "We gave him a faster turnaround and an easier interface," he remembered. "Since we knew the products and services from the technical side and we were creative at heart, we were able to write a better proposal and brochure. And the people reporting to that executive felt like we actually enjoyed helping them, which we did."

Any manager who has dealt with creative types knows the difficulty of getting fast follow-through without a load of grief. Kuroczko found the answer. Show the creative people you like them and they'll move heaven and earth for you (another demonstration of buy-in).

The easiest way to show people you like them is to start with people you can like. Review the chapter "Hire Attitudes Over Experience" for ways to sort through candidates and select individuals who are right for you and your team.

Then, when you have a team you like, make sure they know it. Find ways to tell them you like them and *respect* them.

Kuroczko showed his people he liked them by protecting them. He shielded them from the bank's bureaucracy and spared no effort to make every project fun and rewarding. "I was young and noncorporate. I thought protecting them was being radical," he said. It was radical, but not in the way Kuroczko thought. Every move Kuroczko made to protect his creative band of employees made those team members realize how much they were liked. The employees reciprocated by using all their unconventional skills and exceptional morale to the bank's advantage.

Kelley suggests that managers study teachers of kindergarten-age children. They are constantly showing their classes how much they like them. Next, turn those lessons into adult-appropriate strategies. Take your team on a field trip, or let your people play hooky by going to a movie. At Intel, the bosses always looked for reasons to celebrate—a birthday, the beginning of softball season, a new low in defect rates, or a young engineering tech's last day before college.

Start by liking them. It's a simple but effective way to make a team HOT.

BELIEVE IN THEM.

Anyone can recognize talent and success in hindsight. It's the exceptional manager who will risk their reputation by demonstrating their belief and support for their people before the results are in. But those who take that risk and believe in people learn a valuable lesson—people are more likely to exceed your expectations simply because you believe in them.

Cartoonist Scott Adams learned early in his own career that when someone believes in you, it has an immediate and profound effect on your performance.

> "When I was trying to become a syndicated cartoonist," Adams said (in an article in *Fast Company*), "I sent my portfolio to one cartoon editor after another—and received one rejection after another. One editor even called to suggest that I take art classes."
>
> (Then Sarah Gillespie, an editor at United Syndicate and one of the real experts in the field, called to offer Adams a contract.)
>
> "At first I didn't believe her. I asked if I'd have to change my style, get a partner—or even learn to draw. But she believed that I was already good enough to be a nationally syndicated cartoonist. Her confidence in me completely changed my frame of reference: It altered how I thought about my abilities.
>
> "This may sound bizarre, but from the minute I got off the

phone with her, I could draw better. You can see a marked improvement in the quality of the cartoons I drew after that conversation."

I guess you could call it the power of positive thinking. Again, it's the natural tendency of people to live up to (or down to) your expectations.

"When people feel special," Kelley writes in his book *The Art of Innovation*, "they'll perform beyond your wildest dreams."

You know how good that coach, teacher, relative, or boss who believed in you made you feel. Why not tear a page from their playbook by believing in your own people? It is sure to make your team HOT.

LISTEN TO THEM.

Throughout this book, you've read many reasons for listening better. Listening increases trust, it makes expectations more clear, it relaxes the barriers between people, and it increases self-esteem.

Now here's another reason to make listening a top priority. Listening is one more simple step for making your team HOT.

Dave La Pouple manages a team of twenty salespeople and managers for Clear Channel Communications. He believes listening to associates is the key to his success.

> I've started giving everyone on my subteam, the six people of the twenty that are my direct reports, a weekly one-on-one. That one-on-one allows me to really listen to each person. I force myself, no matter how busy I am, to sit quietly and take a deep breath and pay attention to what my associates are saying. When I shut up and stop everything to listen, they see I'm listening and taking notice of what they are saying. And from there they go out and do better.
>
> I've got one person, with me eighteen months. She came in so unsure of herself. She's had some bad bosses and bad situations. But just by listening every week and saying, "You can do

it," I am reinforcing her belief in herself. It's made her a different person altogether. Listening works.

La Pouple says the challenge of listening is the time it takes. When he started his one-on-ones, they took up the better part of one day out of every week. Now he said he gets a lot more understanding in a lot less time. Still, it's an investment of a manager's most precious resource. But according to La Pouple, "You just have to make it a priority."

MAKE TEAMWORK ENGAGING.
A Stanford professor studied IDEO and found that IDEO employees are more engaged than employees at the average company. "One of the things that's different here [at IDEO] is that at the water cooler and at the company picnic people are actually talking about the work," the professor told Kelley. "It's not like they're people without richness in their lives. They have all these other interests—marathon racing, bicycling, and all that kind of stuff—but they genuinely find the work engaging."

That's no accident, according to Kelley. "Creating a HOT team is about mind-set," he said. "HOT teams don't necessarily have to be organized around the most exciting project. At IDEO, we've developed ways to build teamwork into even the most seemingly ordinary tasks."

One of Kelley's favorite tactics is to create roles for everybody on the team in order to increase their sense of being "chosen." Look around your team to get a sense of the different roles people play, Kelley advised. He suggests that teams assign someone to be the Visionary, the Skeptic, the Technologist, and the Sympathizer, among other characters. Roles, Kelley believes, let people feel special.

Roles also let you use someone for their strengths while avoiding (and protecting them) from their weaknesses.

LET THEM DECIDE.
Kelley admits, "I had to bite my tongue a million times," playing the boss at IDEO. He's worked hard to let teams decide things on their own—as part of making them HOT.

One of Kelley's practices is to let people define their own workspace their own way, within budgets, never allocating space or creating rules about pushpins and posters. He saw the great effects this "let them decide" policy can have one day at one of the IDEO offices.

Kelley was at a weekly meeting of one HOT team when the head of the studio said, "We've got a problem. The studio is booked up solid. We need to add some people, but we're out of room. We made two job offers to associates, and they've both just accepted. These are really good people. We want them to join, but we're out of room. Any ideas?" Kelley bit his tongue to let the team decide.

One guy spoke up. "Everything is on wheels here. If each person gave up one foot of space by the end of the row, we'd have room for one person."

There were two rows of eight cubicles, and so both sides trimmed back one foot so they could accommodate two additional people. Everybody agreed this was the way to solve the problem.

But what impressed Kelley was that everyone willingly gave up a little of their personal space to solve a business problem. "Did everyone get squeezed a little?" Kelley asked. "Yes. But did anyone complain or let that [reduction in the size of their cubicle] get them down? No!"

Giving employees the power to make decisions on their own is the opposite of being rule-bound and hierarchical. And much like believing in people, it has the effect of making people behave more considerately and generously.

A baseball coach explained how giving kids the power made them behave better.

He created a stack of "Get Out of Jail Free" cards for his team. Whenever someone did something he really liked, he would give them a card. Then, whenever they did something he didn't like but they didn't want to be lectured or suffer any other consequences, they could use the card to "get out of jail free." Whenever the coach was presented with the card, he would have to forget that anything bad happened and never mention it.

The results were completely unexpected, he said. The kids did a lot to earn the "Get Out of Jail Free" cards but fewer of the things that would cause them to need the cards. By giving them veto power over a scolding or having to run laps, the team became more mature and better-behaved.

"Kids kept those cards as souvenirs," he remembered.

HOT TEAMS—IMPRACTICAL IDEALISM
OR PRACTICAL PRIORITY?

"Morale is an expression of a work group's emotional health," organizational psychologist Dr. Harry Levinson wrote in his publication *The Levinson Letter*. "High morale is built by managing in such a way that people's psychological needs [as well as their physical needs] are met."

A concerned executive wrote to Levinson in reply: "Yes, all that [about morale] is great, but our managers have to work under heavy pressure to get results." The executive explained to Levinson that perhaps in the future his company's managers could take the time to cultivate such an *ideal* environment, where leaders met the psychological needs of their people in order to create HOT teams. "But today," he told Dr. Levinson, "we can't afford the luxury of such idealism."

I believe that executive was both right and wrong. He was right in his conclusion that good business demands practicality. Every team is under the gun, every manager under pressure. The little room that once was available for wasted time, money, or efforts is gone. We all need to keep our noses to the grindstone.

But Levinson's correspondent was wrong to assume that the activities that turn average work groups into HOT teams are an impractical *luxury*. Let me illustrate why with the following lateral-thinking puzzle:

Bob and Doug are lumberjacks in the Pacific Northwest. They both swing their ax at the exact same rate.

Bob works nonstop from seven in the morning until three-thirty in the afternoon, except for a thirty-minute lunch break.

Doug works the same schedule, but he takes an additional ten-minute break from swinging his ax every hour. That means Doug spends less time cutting trees (six hours and forty minutes a week, to be exact) than Bob.

And yet, at the end of each week, Doug consistently cuts down more trees than Bob. Why?

Lateral-thinking puzzles are designed to help you recognize how many assumptions go into your conclusions. For example, the executive who wrote to Dr. Levinson had concluded that the time spent creating great morale is an idealistic luxury. To reach that conclusion, he has *assumed* that every minute spent doing something other than the primary tasks in the job description (swinging the ax in the tree-cutting business) is a nonproductive minute. Like Bob the lumberjack, he assumes that by keeping his nose (or his people's noses) to the grindstone, he will produce the greatest output.

But the puzzle says that Bob doesn't achieve the best results, Doug does. Why? Doug spends those ten minutes every hour doing something very practical: *sharpening his ax.*

Doug recognized that when you swing your ax all day it tends to get dull, and a dull blade takes longer to cut a tree than a sharp blade. So Doug decided to remove his nose from the grindstone and put his ax blade there instead. As a result, he increased his productivity.

HOT team members want to come to work, enjoy being at work, and would rather work for you than for someone else. That translates into less absenteeism, more initiative, and greater company loyalty, three results that are hardly impractical or idealistic.

What's more, HOT teams feel they can trust management and the company's direction. "They have confidence that the leadership knows where it's going . . . [they] can believe the information they're getting and trust the people who give it to them,"* concludes Dr. Levinson. That translates into the willingness to try new

*Harry Levinson, *Ready, Fire, Aim: Avoiding Management by Impulse,* The Levinson Institute, 1986.

ideas and support changes in direction, creating more *buy-in*. Again, just as buy-in is linked directly to better follow-through, every minute you spend to make your team HOT will make your business better.

Teams with great morale are not a luxury. They are to buy-in and follow-through what Doug's sharper ax is to cutting down more trees—vital.

10 LEAD A HOT TEAM

If you're the one who's responsible for leading a HOT team, I've got some good news and some bad news.

First, here's the bad news. Leading five associates to work together as a HOT team is up to *20 times* more challenging than simply managing a group of five employees. If you add two more people, it becomes 70 times more complex, and if you're responsible for leading a hundred people working as a HOT team, there are almost too many additional complications to imagine (it's beyond 2 to the 99th power).

The good news is, there is a way to successfully manage all the added complexity of getting people to work together as a HOT team, and it doesn't have to cost any more money or take additional hours at work.

Does that sound too good to be true? It won't after you read how a practice leader turned her office of a hundred actuaries and consultants into one of the HOTTEST examples of teamwork on four continents.

But before you read her story, let me explain why leading people to work together as a HOT team is so complicated.

THE CHALLENGE OF TEAMWORK

All goals in business do not require teamwork.

To sell fifty million downloads of digital music, to increase your brand's market share from 10 to 15 percent, to turn around a stagnant business unit, or to achieve any other big objective in business, a manager must get many different people to do their personal best. But simply because a lot of people contribute to the outcome, it doesn't mean that the goal depends on teamwork.

Teamwork is essential when the group's big objective has a high degree of what experts call "task interdependency." Task interdependency measures just how much the action of any single person influences the success of another employee and the team's overall results.

Getting an airplane off the ground on time requires more than a dozen different people, performing many distinct tasks, very quickly, under changing conditions, to pull together and work as a team. It's a highly interdependent process.

Booking someone's travel plans also requires the work of dozens of different people. But as the timing is spread out and coordination is not as critical, each person can work as an individual. It's not a highly interdependent process.

In general, when people can do their jobs with their heads down—giving each task their best individual effort, but with little concern about the impact of their decisions or personal style on other workers—and the group can still hit their big objective, that group's goals have a low degree of task interdependence and teamwork is not especially important.

On the other hand, when the individual's willingness to look beyond their self-interests and coordinate, cooperate, and communicate with many other employees makes or breaks the team's success, task interdependence is high and teamwork is absolutely vital.

It's the need to help people recognize the effect of their decisions and work style on others and to readily adapt as circumstances change that makes leading HOT teams much more complicated. The reason is obvious.

Teamwork is a choice employees make based on how they feel. Those feelings are the result of how each member of the team *relates* day-to-day.

When relationships are poor, people are uninterested in the impact of their decisions and work style on others and unwilling to extend any extra effort to pull together as a team. They are more rigid, insensitive, and self-centered.

When the relationships are good, team members coordinate, cooperate, and communicate without prompting and quickly adjust to the situations at hand with an eye toward achieving the team's big objective. They are more pliant, empathetic, and generous.

So when tasks are interdependent and success requires teamwork, it's the leader's responsibility to make sure there are good relationships between all the teammates. That can look like a relatively small challenge, resting on the leader's people-management skills, but it's bigger than that. When you add up all the relationships and imagine the impact of any potential conflicts, it's clear that unless your teams are small there are too many relationships for one person to manage.

THE SPAN OF RELATIONSHIPS IN A HOT TEAM

Say Ellyn is leading a team of five, including Holly, Steve, Kelly, Debbie, and Mary. If the group has objectives that don't include a lot of task interdependencies, Ellyn has to manage just five relationships; Ellyn and Holly, Ellyn and Steve, Ellyn and Kelly, and so on.

But if her group's goals hinge on how well the team coordinates, cooperates, and communicates with one another, Ellyn has to manage those same five direct relationships, plus worry about twenty peer-to-peer relationships (Holly and Steve, Holly and Kelly, Holly and Debbie, and so on in both directions) and seventy-five combinations of peers and leadership (Ellyn and Holly with Steve present, Ellyn and Steve with Holly and Kelly present, and so on). Altogether there are one hundred different combinations, or *twenty times more relationships* for Ellyn to manage than if she were simply trying to get five individuals to do their personal best.

That total number of relationships increases exponentially. If Ellyn adds two associates to her team for a total of seven (one to seven was the 2001 average manager-to-employee ratio in business), she has a team with 490 different relationships. If her group grows to 100, she'll find, to her surprise, more than 2 to the 99th power of possible relationships between associates and managers.

Now, before you dismiss the influence of all these potential relationships as insignificant, think about the last time you had jury duty or served as the leader of a committee.

- Do you remember the profound effect different people had on group dynamics?
- Did you notice how different parts of the group would gang up and influence one person?
- Did you ever find yourself shaking your head at how some small slight between participants got blown out of proportion?
- Did you notice how payback for any real or imagined slights occurred unexpectedly and at the worst possible moment?

In fact, as panels convene to understand the causes of disasters (like 9/11) and horrible accidents (like the 1986 Space Shuttle *Challenger* explosion), they have found that relationships are more at fault than dereliction of duty or gross incompetence. In the 1986 Challenger incident, experts concluded, it was the many flawed interactions between teams at NASA and Morton Thiokol (the maker of the *Challenger*'s rockets and installer of the failed O-rings) that contributed to the decision to launch the shuttle despite very cold conditions. They determined that imperfect relationships between well-intentioned managers, executives, and engineers at both organizations led to blind spots and groupthink.

Managers who need people to pull together to deal effectively with task interdependencies are left with one of three choices. Either they can ignore the obvious, leave group relationships to chance, and let problems turn into disasters, or they can break the bank to hire and train enough supervision to help resolve all the possible conflicts, or they can follow a leader who found a way to get more than a hundred associates to foster better relationships on their own and become one of the HOTTEST teams of all her company's many international locations.

THE SOLUTION

Elizabeth "Buffy" Caflisch is a practice leader (and a former member of the board of directors) at Watson Wyatt, one of the big international consulting firms. Her Washington, D.C., office specializes in helping Fortune 500 client firms follow through on the retirement benefits they've promised to their employees.

Caflisch didn't set out to improve the relationships in her office of a hundred actuaries and consultants. She was just trying to make sure she was following through on her personal mission. "It is my responsibility to see that we are helping each associate learn and grow," she said. "There were days when I thought the way we led the practice was working well, and then there were the days that I wondered *was I really following through like I should*?"

Caflisch knew exactly what she'd like to have happen. She wanted to "encourage rapid growth and development," and have her associates "discover the mixture of roles that made work most satisfying." In essence, Caflisch wanted to *coach* each of her one hundred associates to their full potential.

But that wasn't going to be possible. Caflisch's first duty is to her clients. She spends almost a third of her time directly addressing their problems and devising great solutions. Plus, as the D.C. practice leader, she is responsible for all the goals of a general manager—juggling headquarters' demands for tight expense control and to aggressively improve both productivity and profitability.

Coaching a hundred associates to their full potential requires a lot of feedback, mentoring, and planning—activities that, when a manager is determined to do each well, take thousands of hours Caflisch knew she didn't have.

Then inspiration hit. "Happily," she explained, "[I realized that] many people felt like there was something significant they could do to take us forward. They wanted to contribute in a way that let them stay on the consulting track and still help out. I decided that if I gave those people a way to make a contribution in a way they were most comfortable making it, we'd all be stronger for it."

So instead of wishing she had more time to coach each person to their full potential, Caflisch distributed the responsibility among her team members. Specifically, she implemented a system whereby about one-third of the Washington, D.C., practice assumed the role of "buddy," coach, or team advisor, and the entire office took charge of providing every associate with timely, specific, and useful performance feedback.

Buddies

The buddy's job is to show a new person the ropes—to share the knowledge they need to get things done—and to fully integrate him into the processes and culture of the office. The buddy is expected to provide on-the-job training, teaching him everything she knows in order to supplement the practice's formal training program.

"We pair the new person with a buddy one rung higher," Caflisch said. It's a full-year commitment for one-on-one assistance. "The idea is that by the end of that first twelve months the buddy has transferred their knowledge and responsibilities to the new person."

Caflisch explained the value of this system. "Buddies understand that the better they train their replacement, the more opportunity they will have to advance." The buddy knows it's their mission to see that their protégé is fully capable of taking over their duties.

Coaches

The second part of Caflisch's distributed-leadership initiative is a comprehensive coaching arrangement. "There's one coach for every seven to ten people," Caflisch said. "He or she is typically one or two bands ahead of the coachee." (Watson Wyatt has six bands of associates, each band representing a different level of experience.)

The coach is responsible for listening to the associates' challenges, providing advice about appropriate training, steering them to the right client assignments, giving them the feedback from peers, bosses, and subordinates, and delivering the yearly performance appraisals. Everyone at every level of the practice has a coach.

Coaches devote about 15 percent of their workweek guiding other members of the practice. "Many people want to contribute to the practice in a way that lets them stay on the consulting track," Caflisch explained. "This allows them to try their hand at leadership."

Team Advisors

The goal of the client team advisor is to make sure each member of the team is learning new skills and gaining new competencies as fast as they can.

The position of client team advisor was created in response to the typical organizational urge to assign everything to someone who has done it before. "Sometimes, if you are under pressure, the easy way out is to assign the person to things they have done before," Caflisch observed. "Someone needs to say, 'Wait, we need other people to learn to do this.'"

"You've never done this before," a client team advisor might say to an associate, "but it is important that you understand this aspect of our work. I'm going to find you an opportunity." Caflisch concluded, "It's best for everyone if we stretch and help associates gain new competencies."

Each advisor meets individually to discuss the associate's next-year and long-term plan. Then they decide how the team can help support those objectives by mixing and matching the work assignments on each team for the upcoming year.

For example, "Perhaps an associate has never worked directly advising a client," Caflisch said. "If on their long-term plan they intend to grow to consultant status, a client team advisor needs to involve the associate in conference calls, meetings, and other client communications during the year. That way they can begin to hear about client assignments from the client's point of view and observe experienced consultants diagnosing and leading those efforts to help clients address their business issues."

360-Degree Feedback

Through her system of 360-degree feedback, Caflisch gets every person in her office to share in the responsibilities of leading people to reach their full potential.

"Feedback sources in the Washington, D.C., office include associates for whom you work, with whom you work, and who do work for you, as well as a self-assessment," Caflisch explained. "We like to hear from five to seven teammates, each carefully selected by the associate in agreement with the coach so that the feedback gathered touches on all of the associate's key responsibilities and performance levels throughout the year."

Caflisch challenges each source to do more than provide an opinion.

"Please take the time to think through your comments carefully," she advises all the associates. "Include specific examples to help the coach understand your comments."

- What is the nature of your work with the associate?
- What were your expectations of the associate's work?
- How well did the associate meet your expectations?
- On what areas should the associate focus in order to expand the range and value of his future contributions?
- If you have any ideas for an action plan, list them here.

According to Caflisch, her 360-degree feedback system works on the natural urge of everyone to "add their own touch to shaping and improving the future path of the business . . . making it a place where *they* want to work."

Caflisch's process of distributing the leadership does more than give her a helping hand in fulfilling her mission, providing each associate with the one-on-one attention they need to keep learning and growing. This process improves all the interpersonal relationships without any extra expense or one additional hour of Caflisch's time (than she would have spent using conventional hierarchical leadership).

Think about it. Whom (in business) do you implicitly trust? Who has earned your friendship? Who could get your complete cooperation just by asking? Most people in business have a special place in their hearts for those associates and supervisors who gave them useful feedback and took enough interest to coach them in their careers. At Watson Wyatt's Washington, D.C., practice each consultant and actuary sees an office full of those kinds of devoted mentors supporting each team member. It's an environment that compels cooperation.

Now look from the other side. Who has your fondest hopes for their future success? Who gets your most patient understanding when confused or wrongheaded? Where are the empathetic bonds the strongest? Again, most people in business feel something special about their eager protégés and enthusiastic students. And again, Caflisch's team members make that connection with others from the first year they join the practice.

The result (as you'll read in a moment) is that looking out for number one and ignoring the impact of one's decisions and personal style on others is discouraged without anyone's saying a word. Communication, cooperation, and coordination become the default response to task interdependencies, and great relationships are forged throughout the practice.

THE RESULT

Shortly after introducing distributed leadership to the practice, Caflisch saw its amazing effect on relationships and a team's ability to successfully manage task interdependencies, even in difficult circumstances.

"We were about to begin a huge assignment for an important client," Caflisch recalled. It was a comprehensive, top-to-bottom review that required Watson Wyatt's analysts to juggle a massive amount of data, crunch the numbers on lots of possible scenarios, and respond quickly to many "what if" questions. She was stressed.

It wasn't the scale or the speed of this project that concerned Caflisch. Her office had excellent quality assurance, and the Washington, D.C., staff had successfully completed this same type of review many times in the past.

Caflisch was nervous because, for the first time, the vast majority of the associates assigned to follow through on this complex and time-critical analysis would be new to their roles.

"One of our most qualified team members had just retired, and another transferred to a new office," Caflisch explained. "So out of nine people on the team, *seven* were out of college five years or less." Imagine if 77 percent of the people you needed on a critical mission under a very tight deadline were new and you can see why Caflisch spent a few restless nights and anxious days.

But before she had a chance to share her concerns or call a meeting to discuss some stopgap measures, that team showed Caflisch she had nothing to worry about.

"Within days of starting the project, the team took stock of the unique challenges of this important project," Caflisch said, "and created their own solution."

They first divided the workload by the specific kinds of expertise necessary to reliably complete each phase of the project. Then, instead of just handing off the responsibility to the teammate with the most experience and giving low-level assignments to the new associates in a kind of hierarchy, they paired themselves up, with a more experienced analyst working shoulder-to-shoulder with each junior associate. (In other words, associates with a year of experience were paired with someone with a couple of years under their belt, and so on.)

Their process was simple. The experienced person *did the job* while the junior person observed and asked questions. Then the junior person took a turn while the more experienced person coached them one-on-one. Within a few cycles, every junior person was completely up to speed and able to handle the new responsibilities on her own. The "coach" then could move on to tackle the next part of the analysis and be coached herself as she expanded her proficiency.

"I was totally in awe of what they accomplished," Caflisch said proudly. Despite the fact that seven out of nine team members were new to many of the critical tasks, she observed, "we were further ahead and better able to respond to our client's requests than we'd ever been before." In other words, the new team equaled the performance of a much more seasoned group.

This team's superb performance was the result of the way the associates related to one another. "They were more prepared, the whole team understood better what to do, and they were faster to respond because," Caflisch concluded, "the team chose to *share their knowledge* without reservation. I was amazed."

Unrestrained knowledge sharing, people looking out for one another rather than sitting on their hands, everyone buying in to the group's big objective and going above and beyond to follow through—this is the level of teamwork we all dream of.

But it doesn't have to be a dream.

The obstacles to teamwork are significant. There are innumerable task interdependencies and countless interactions. Any crack among all the relationships could cause your follow-through to fail. When you do the math and compare the time and attention it could take, the complications will appear to be overwhelming.

But if you can see in your staff the willingness of each person to (as Caflisch put it) "add their own touch to shaping and improving the future path of the business," and focus that drive, turning it into coaching and providing helpful feedback, the result will be naturally improved relationships and teamwork.

So the answer to the question "How do you lead a HOT team?" is "You don't." Distribute the coaching responsibilities of leadership and your HOT team members will lead themselves.

GOOD FEEDBACK

At the heart of any coaching relationship is good feedback.

But when you think about the pointers you've received and (if you're candid) the advice you've given, it's clear most feedback isn't very good.

That's not because businesspeople are too self-centered or shy to provide a constructive critique. They simply haven't thought it through.

So let me give you some feedback on giving good feedback:

Imagine twelve people are evenly divided into three teams.

Each group is told to choose one person, to blindfold them, and to give that teammate a five-inch rubber ball. Then they are to point the "shooter" in the right direction and instruct him or her to toss that ball into a trash can ten feet away.

"Each team will be given ten shots," they are told. "The goal is to make the most baskets."

The first group is restricted from saying anything or touching their blindfolded teammate until he has completed all ten tries. They wait until the round is over and then give their shooter some specific feedback, such as "Your first shot was long and left, the next fell short . . . ," and so on.

The second group is allowed to talk to the shooter all they want, but they must restrict their comments to phrases like "Good job" or "Keep trying—we believe in you." During their round, they offer the shooter lots of encouraging words and nothing more.

The third group was given no restrictions. They did what came naturally. During their round, they gave their shooter detailed instructions about how and where the last lob missed, and offered advice about force, trajectory, and direction. They even took some time for questions from the blindfolded teammate.

Now, as you imagine the scene, consider your answers to these three questions:

1. At the end of the complete first round, which team would likely have the best results?
2. How about at the end of a second round?
3. Lastly, which blindfolded team member would be the most enthusiastic about being handed the ball for a second or third round?

Your answers tell you all you need to know about creating a framework for good feedback.

The first group represents the year-end-performance-review school of feedback. It's not good feedback because it was delayed.

The second group symbolizes the *self-esteem* school of feedback. It's not good because it is vague.

It's the third group that represents good feedback. Why? Because their comments are timely and specific.

Timely. It takes about 440 pounds of protein, carbs, fat, and fiber to sustain the average person for a year. But no one would think they could save time by eating it all at one sitting. To sustain life, food needs to be spread out over the year.

Feedback is the same. All year long, people need to adjust, tune, get refreshed, and put things in their proper perspective. Feedback won't do that if you get it in one big dose with the year-end perfor-mance review. "The sooner someone gets the recognition that they did a great job or hears what they did that didn't work too well for the team," Caflisch learned, "the more clearly they know how to approach the next project," which will bring even better results.

Specific. Forty assembled managers were asked, "What are the qualities that you want from a leader?" After reciting a long list of all the things they probably heard in workshops—confidence, charisma, integrity, communication skills, persistence, a vision, blah, blah, blah—each was asked to reconsider. "If you needed to cross a minefield and someone said, 'Hey, everybody, go this way,' would it matter if they had charisma, a vision, confidence, or any of that other stuff?"

"Not really," they said. "The most important thing would be for them to *point out* the right way to go." That's what people really want from feedback, not inspiration or motivation but specifics from someone who has honestly taken the time to understand which path is best.

That puts the pressure for good feedback right where it belongs—on the source. It's not good enough just to share an opinion—feed-back needs to be filled with specific and helpful information.

Two disciplines will help you make all feedback specific:

1. Sources must give feedback in writing. (As we learned in "More Accurate Assessments," writing answers has a profound effect on the quality of thinking that goes into each response.)

2. Sources must get feedback on their feedback. Caflisch learned

the importance of getting feedback when it was pointed out that her group's rating system was inconsistent. "With so many raters," Caflisch realized, "it's hard to get everybody on the same scale." So now Caflisch meets with all coaches to come up with consistent ratings. "We talk through all the levels of performance together to work out our definitions. What does it mean, specifically, to have a 'good solid year' in comparison to someone who 'blew out the lights'? How does someone who 'met expectations' differ specifically from someone who didn't?" That never would have happened if Caflisch wasn't open to feedback herself.

Building Block IV

■

INDIVIDUAL INITIATIVE

So far we've examined three major obstacles to making sure what's expected gets done (the definition of following through from a manager's perspective):

- The debilitating effect that vague or conflicting goals and flawed assessments can have on knowing what's expected.
- How a manager cuts the odds of getting things done in half by failing to match the right people to their goals.
- And the instinctive resistance that keeps people from buying in to any changes in direction or following through on new ideas.

For each of these obstructions (and every bump in between), we've gotten insights from a business leader who has faced the challenge head-on and found a solution.

Now you have the tools to make sure your people follow through—*what to do* to give everyone a crystal-clear direction, how to find the best fit between your people and goals, and the steps to take that will guarantee your people get off to a great start.

Yet it's still not enough. Despite all your best efforts, much of what you expect your people to get done can still fall through the cracks . . . simply from a lack of individual initiative.

Let me paint you a picture.

WHERE'S THEIR INITIATIVE? #1

Nick was checking in at United Airlines' first-class counter.

The agent had just handed him his boarding pass and was tagging his luggage. Nick noticed she wasn't using the yellow first-class flags on his luggage. He asked why. "I'm out of those tags," the agent said without looking up. "These [red, business class] flags will have to do. Thank you."

Nick glanced over to the next agent, not three feet away, and saw a big stack of the yellow first-class tags. He leaned forward and said quietly, "There's a stack by that agent." Nick nodded toward her associate.

The woman looked up, stared at Nick for a second, and forced her tiniest smile, stating, "I already said thank you." Then she called out to the line behind him, "NEXT!"

It was a moment right out of a *Seinfeld* episode. Nick had just been "Soup Nazied" by United Airlines. He made a point of not flying United for the next year.

WHERE'S THEIR INITIATIVE? #2

Joe is a top performer in the personal investor group at a big bank. His employer paid him very well and regularly rewarded Joe with bonuses and trips to tropical locations.

As part of a new growth initiative, HR met with each of the bank's best brokers and encouraged them to spend a year training for an advanced certification in investment planning. "We're installing new technology to help you service high net-worth individuals," they told Joe. "Your part is to train and pass the exams. By the time you finish, we'll have the equipment installed. And then we'll have an unbeatable new service."

Joe was enthused. He started the training immediately and aced all the tests. Certification in hand, Joe waited for the new computers and the promised software . . . and waited and waited.

Nothing ever came, and nobody ever explained why.

Last summer, another bank offered Joe a big bonus if he'd cross over and work for them. It was an offer he couldn't (and didn't) refuse. When his group manager said good-bye he told Joe, with the real regret every manager feels when they lose a top performer, "I wish there were something I could do to keep you."

WHERE'S THEIR INITIATIVE? #3

All the senior executives at a big national media company agreed to spend one day a month getting close to the customer.

In September, a senior vice president went to see clients with the local managers from his local affiliate. His day ended at one of their largest new accounts, a LASIK surgery center.

The visiting executive poured on the charm, and the client loved the attention. In closing, he leaned forward and said to the LASIK center's director, "I want to send you something that will shed more light on the things we've been discussing."

Nothing ever arrived.

Twelve months later, at that same center, the client reminded the local sales manager of that encounter as she explained why she chose another outlet for the upcoming year's ad buy. "You guys are all the same," she concluded in a tone that showed some real damage had been done. "Nobody follows through anymore."

You could argue that communicating more clearly about the organization's direction, finding a better fit (by hiring people who won't drop the ball), or smoothing the way for follow-through (perhaps by increasing the buy-in) would cure the breakdowns in each of these three stories. But that analysis would miss the point.

- Considering the fix the U.S. carriers were in, long before 9/11, that United Airlines first-class ticket agent *had to understand* how important every customer was to United, especially first-class customers and frequent flyers. Nick was both—a 100,000 mile (1K) flyer who flew business or first class for every trip. That made him one of the 9 percent of passengers who generated 46 percent of the carrier's revenues. The agent knew that—Nick was in the first-class line, his 1K status was on the computer screen before her, and United had been working with front-line employees on customer service for years. Everything that agent needed for meeting Nick's expectations was within arm's reach. All she really lacked was the initiative.

- When circumstances force a company to delay or break a commitment to an employee (as they did at Joe's bank), you'd better give him or her a good explanation, quickly. Otherwise, he'll imagine the worst. HR knows that. They also know that the cost of replacing a top producer is really high—you run the risk of replacing him with someone who can't deliver the same results and face the likelihood that some valuable accounts will defect along with him. Yet nobody at that bank did anything to reassure one of their top producers and they lost him to a rival institution. What was missing? Their initiative.

- When the promised "something" never arrived from the regional VP, the manager of that LASIK surgery center was disappointed. That disappointment sparked her curiosity ("I wonder if there's a better media outlet for my ad dollars?") and opened the door to a competitor's inducement ("The other people have offered a cheaper price," she thought. "I might as well save some money, since they're all the same.") Everyone in sales and marketing knows a disappointed customer is much more likely to defect and that finding replacement customers is extremely expensive. But the VP *and* the local managers still let their promise fall through the cracks. (The local managers could have reminded the VP of his promise or connected with his personal assistant to get something that would satisfy the client.) Again, all that was missing was individual initiative.

HOW CAN YOU GUARANTEE MORE INITIATIVE?

Conventional wisdom says the way to get more individual initiative is for managers to emphasize individual accountability (by developing programs like MAPS—minimum acceptable performance standards) and apply significant consequences for poor performance (like dismissing the poorest-performing 5 to 10 percent of employees each year). But, as we've seen in many of the examples in this book, *conventional wisdom can often be wrong.*

According to the managers and organizations profiled throughout this book, strict accountability and hard-nosed consequences *are not* effective strategies for getting individuals and groups to show enough initiative.

INITIATIVE AT IKEA

IKEA is a $12-billion global business. In 2002, they were the top retailer on the Google *Zeitgeist* (the top retail name among billions of queries made using the Google search system). IKEA was also the number-five brand on Google's list, right behind Disney and ahead of Dell and Microsoft. With only fourteen stores in the United States, IKEA was (in 2002) the seventh-largest volume seller of furniture, bedding, and accessories in America. During 2003 they opened nine new stores, and by 2007 IKEA will have a total of fifty locations in North America. They expect to be number one in their industry by then.

Some of IKEA's success is due to their enlightened supply-chain management. The company partners with their sources, sharing know-how and capital generously to get the lowest cost of goods and the leanest, most responsive manufacturing and distribution. Some of their success is due to their empathic connection with their customers. Their design teams stay very close to real people, regularly reading between the lines and surprising customers with the perfect balance between a product that solves one of life's challenges inexpensively and one that delights the senses. And some of their success is the result of their unique style of promotion and marketing. But none of the company's success would be possible without an uncommon level of initiative, shown by IKEA associates in every function.

Take IKEA's marketing and promotions department, for example. IKEA doesn't rely solely on their quirky TV commercials, four-color catalogs, or big newspaper ads to promote their $12-billion business. Half of their ad budget is spent in the stores, where teams of full-time interior designers, visual merchandisers, builders, and graphic artists create dozens of lifestyle solutions that promote the IKEA brand as well as specific products and events.

"IKEA needs to communicate a new life, a new way of living. So we look for dilemmas faced by real people in real homes," said Lena Simonson-Berge, the North American Director of Marketing for IKEA. "For example, we might imagine a woman and her daughter in a small apartment. Life presents them with challenges. How can they get a great place to entertain friends and family, to do homework, and simply enjoy each day with only 705 square feet and spending less than $4,600 to completely furnish two bedrooms, a dining area, and a family room?" To get answers to questions like these, Simonson-Berge's goal is to turn each store into a discovery center where shoppers experience IKEA's unique style, innovative thinking, and low prices.

The marketing teams start by doing a lot of homework—talking with and observing actual customers in actual situations. Then they brainstorm solutions and draw up their designs. After getting input and critiques from the store and product teams, each store's group will build a fully functional, three-dimensional concept room demonstrating IKEA's best new product ideas. Each store does thirty-five of these a year, every one a unique example of IKEA's branding message, executed with the care and attention to detail worthy of a Disneyland display.

When you do the math, you get an idea how much IKEA's marketing relies on each associate showing enough initiative.

There are eighteen stores, each with their own group of twenty creative personalities, all of them generating thirty-five full-scale solutions each year. That's 360 full-time people undertaking six hundred and thirty major initiatives. Each solution requires several days of research, imaginative thinking, and prototyping as well as time for construction and finish work. In keeping with the IKEA way of doing things, each team member is very passionate and intelligent, focused on the diverse needs in *their* market and the priorities of *their* store. Add to this mix the IKEA guiding principle that everything gets done with "small means" (the tightest possible budget in the often extravagant marketing business) and you have a huge scope of activity, potential conflict, and expectations to manage.

Yet according to Simonson-Berge, all the follow-through at IKEA gets done without a lot of pushing or prodding by management.

What kind of follow-up systems does IKEA use?

"We don't use a strict supervision system to make sure our people follow through," Simonson-Berge explained. "Each [associate] is very concerned about what they do and about their contribution. We just trust them."

The president of the North American Division, Pernille Spiers-Lopez, said much the same thing as she explained the follow-through it took to open more new stores in just eight months of 2003 than IKEA had ever opened before.

"Why should we put all kinds of stuff in place to follow up? We have found it is better to let people go," Spiers-Lopez said. "As long as we have competent people and we give them the right prerequisites—the information, the knowledge, and the tools—we can trust that they will get the job done without any prodding or pushing."

But other companies have competent people who've been given clear direction, a good plan, and all the resources, and still their people fail to show enough initiative. What is different at IKEA?

"I don't know exactly," Spiers-Lopez said when asked this question. "It [follow-through] just happens . . . naturally. We found if someone has the passion and leadership facilitates the right conditions, there's nothing stopping them."

"We communicate, we network, and we're humanistic," Simonson-Berge added, trying to explain the IKEA way. "We have values. It's just that simple."

IS THE ANSWER THAT SIMPLE?

A book on follow-through can't throw out vague concepts like "passion" and "the *right* conditions," along with general directives like "have values" and "be humanistic." After all, according to the first building block of follow-through, clear direction, ambiguity is why so many expectations aren't met. I wanted specific answers from IKEA—how to generate this *passion*, what constitutes the *right* conditions, what are the values that drive *initiative*, and how a business manager balances *humanism* with competitiveness.

Unfortunately, those specifics were something IKEA executives couldn't detail except in general terms.

But just because a manager can't give a specific explanation of *what they do* doesn't mean they don't do specific things. It's likely that the strategies and tactics that IKEA uses are so embedded in the IKEA culture that they seem to be a part of the environment, something the managers don't have to think about, like year-round climate control or 24/7 lighting in the stores.

So instead of asking them for specifics, we need to use our intuition, just as we would with a boss who offered us vague goals and wasn't clear. We need to read between the lines.

Look closely at what Simonson-Berge said and you can begin to crack the code.

1. *Each [IKEA associate] is very concerned about what they do and about their contribution.*

   People can choose whether or not to put their hearts into what they do. You can't force them. Leadership has to decide if they are going to build their business around people who do just what's necessary to keep the boss off their back or find the kinds of people and follow the specific practices that make sure people will put their heart into following through. Many companies do the former; IKEA does the latter.

2. *We're humanistic.*

   Merriam-Webster's online dictionary defines humanism as a way of life centered on values, especially stressing an individual's dignity, worth, and capacity for self-realization. This is a fundamental issue for leaders at every level. Quite often, dignity, worth, and concern for personal growth are missing in conventional management tactics. Most companies have the attitude "It's a dog-eat-dog world and we'll get more humanistic when things calm down." But IKEA balances their need for intensity and competitiveness with extraordinarily *humane* principles, finding the line between what encourages and what kills their associates' initiative and working hard not to cross it. (We've examined this already in "Create a HOT Team" and will add more in "Find the Line Between Enough and Too Much Accountability.")

3. *We just trust them.* Once the passion, competence, concern, desire to make a contribution, and the belief that what your team does *matters*, is encouraged in the everyday environment of their businesses, managers need to do their job in a way that shows they trust their people. This is the biggest difference at IKEA compared to most other companies. Many managers fall back on tactics of authoritarian control because their mental models say they can't trust their employees. IKEA executives have a different perspective and act accordingly.

INITIATIVE CAN BE NATURAL

Mel Haught, CEO of Pella Corporation (introduced in the chapter "Get Everyone to 'Just Let Go'"), agrees with Simonson-Berge and Spiers-Lopez of IKEA. "We forget that the same people we are around at work go home and build the new church, remodel the schoolroom, help a neighbor fix their car, organize the Heart Association's local fund-raising, all on their own [without the pushing and prodding of managers]," said Haught, whose company is one of the most productive manufacturers in America. "We just need to unleash and focus those same motivations in their work."

Joanne Lipman of the *Wall Street Journal;* Bill Zollars of Yellow Roadway Corporation; James Crowe, the CEO of Level 3 Communication; Richard Coraine of the Union Square Hospitality Group; Tom Kelley of IDEO; Linda Lockwood of Charles Schwab; and Sister Mary Jean Ryan of the Baldrige Award winner SSM Health Care—all those who've shared their insights and tools for improving follow-through—agree with Haught and the managers at IKEA.

They all practice strategies and tactics to unleash and focus initiative rather than relying on pushing and prodding.

How can a manager inspire those motivations? Through extensive research, lengthy conversations, and observations of the managers at IKEA and all the other companies featured in this book, three specific management strategies have surfaced. Each plays a crucial role in supporting individual initiative.

They are:
• Share Your Purpose
• Show More Respect
• Find the Line Between Enough and Too Much Accountability

11 SHARE YOUR PURPOSE

■

We don't work in a perfect world. There's always something that gets in the way, a stumbling block we didn't see coming.

This means managers need to do more than anticipate and clear the obstacles to following through. Leaders must help their people focus on a *reason* to rise above tough conditions and take the initiative necessary to make sure what's expected gets done. That challenge forces managers to consider a few fundamental questions about human nature.

- *What compels people to overcome adversity?*
- *What causes average people to stare down difficult or even impossible circumstances and put all their heart into following through?*
- *What do some individuals have that drives them to take a deep breath and power through any sticking points while others are more easily derailed?*

In the 1990s, business executives thought they had found the answer. Companies began to give stock grants and options to all employees instead of only to the senior executives, figuring that making employees owners would get them to "take ownership."

Yet even at the height of the stock market bubble, Gallup's Curt Coffman, coauthor of *First Break All the Rules*, reported that 71 percent of all workers were not fully engaged; many were just clock watchers who couldn't wait to go home. Today that statistic is relatively unchanged.

Clearly, managers need something more than money to get their people so thoroughly engaged that they would persist in following through under less-than-perfect circumstances.

Shakespeare pointed to one solution. As you read between the lines of the text in which he dramatized the battle between the French and the English at Agincourt, you can see that one sure way to get people to rise above difficulties and show enough initiative is to share a purpose.

SHAKESPEARE AND SHARED PURPOSE

The scene is a soldier's camp at dawn on a cold October day in 1415. The English troops are worn out after long days of marching. They are nervous, knowing the other side outnumbers them six to one. As they look past their camp to the field of battle, they see an ocean of knee-deep mud. Someone wishes aloud that the conditions were better and that some of their countrymen who stayed behind in England were with them there to fight.

King Henry, realizing that his only chance of winning the battle was to get each man and boy to overcome the harsh conditions and show uncommon initiative, hears this comment and reacts.

"No," he says so all the troops can hear, "wish not one man more." Why? Henry explains that his purpose is to be honored, and the fewer men there to fight, he argues, "the greater [his] share of honor." He then tells all his troops that he will gratefully share this honor with each of them. And he paints a persuasive picture of how that day's honor will set each of them apart from all those who chose to stay safe at home:

We few, we happy few, we band of brothers;
For he today who sheds his blood with me
Shall be my brother; be he ne'er so vile,
this day shall gentle his condition
and gentlemen in England, now abed,
shall think themselves accursed they were not here
And hold their manhood's cheap while any speaks
That fought with us . . .

Under impossible circumstances—outnumbered, outresourced, and with no reasonable expectation of success—Henry and his band of brothers battled at Agincourt. Despite the awful conditions and enormous odds, Henry's purpose gave each English soldier the initiative they needed. At the end of the day, the French were defeated.

Shakespeare's conclusion is clear: Shared purpose is a force that compels people to swell up and follow through with all their heart.

SHARED PURPOSE IN THE FIREHOUSE

A current-day example of the power of shared purpose is on display inside any firehouse.

"What sets the firefighter apart," explained New York's First Deputy Fire Commissioner William Freehan, "it's he or she who [when the bell sounds] has to go into harm's way and do whatever is necessary to help."

The late commissioner was interviewed in 1992 on the factors that compel fire and rescue workers to rush into disasters as others are running away. His interview is part of the official Fire Department of New York's tribute to the 343 firefighters (including Freehan himself) who made the supreme sacrifice on 9/11. What's remarkable about his eloquent comments is how closely they parallel Shakespeare's insights from four hundred years earlier.

- *Fire and rescue workers share a purpose that's bigger than themselves.* Henry's soldiers fought for honor; Freehan's people are fighting to help others. "The whole department exists," Freehan said of the 16,330 firefighters, rescue workers, officers, marshals, inspectors, and support personnel that make up the FDNY, "to serve the people of the city. I know . . . that sounds corny, but that's the reason."

- *That purpose can't be measured in dollars and cents.* History is clear: The mercenary doesn't stand a chance against the purpose-driven combatant. Henry told his soldiers, "I do not covet gold." The same thing is true in the firehouse. "I don't think you can pay people to do that job, to go to the aid of a stranger even when it means that you may put yourself in dire peril," Freehan explained. "There has to be something beyond money."

- *Initiative will be rewarded with meaningful recognition.* Henry told his troops their efforts will make them immortal. "We shall be remembered," the king said. The same is true at the Fire Department of New York. "We have a memorial day," Freehan continued. "We go up to the fireman's monument on 100th Street and honor all those firefighters who died in the last year either in the line of duty or through natural causes. We have this every single year."

Shared purpose compels initiative whether you're fighting fires or a nation's enemies. But what about in business? Can sharing a purpose drive follow-through in more routine situations?

SHARED PURPOSE AT IKEA

It's been said that IKEA founder Ingvar Kamprad had nothing but two empty hands when he set out to build his global home-furnishings business. It's true—he had no inheritance, no loans, and no preexisting resources available to fund his dream. But Kamprad was far from being empty-handed. He had energy, imagination, and a powerful desire to prove himself. He also had a *purpose.*

"You must have noticed that it is not easy to make ends meet," Kamprad wrote to customers in 1949. "Why is this? You yourself produce goods of various kinds (milk, grain, potatoes, etc.), and I suppose you do not receive too much payment for them. No, I am sure you don't. Yet everything is so fantastically expensive. To a great extent, this is due to the middlemen. We have taken a step in the right direction by offering you goods at the same prices your dealer buys for, in some cases even lower."

Those thoughts were refined to articulate a purpose that guided Kamprad and his early employees. "IKEA," Kamprad declared emphatically, *"will create a better everyday life for the majority of people."*

Kamprad's purpose is something IKEA executives refer to as they explain their natural way of generating initiative. "IKEA is not what it is because of a small group of people, sitting on the top of a hill somewhere. IKEA is the success it is because of our people," Marketing Director Lena Simonson-Berge explained. "Each is, to one degree or another, very passionate about the business idea."

That business idea, as Kamprad set it up half a century ago, is to enable the majority of people to have a more pleasant and convenient existence than would be possible without IKEA. It inspires buyers, designers, and managers to take the initiative and approach their jobs with creativity and originality.

- "We don't buy products," IKEA's buyers say, "we buy production capabilities. We look for unconventional sources, like using a ski supplier to make tables or a shirt manufacturer with excess capacity to make cushions." Why? So they can get a lot more for their money than the traditional furniture buyer. That is how they share in Kamprad's purpose.

- Their shared purpose continually challenges the designers at IKEA. "Why does good-looking, functional furniture have to be expensive?" an IKEA designer will ask him- or herself. "Any designer can create a table that costs $700, but only the best can do one for $70." So the products they make bring the beauty and quality of more expensive designs for a price that average people can easily afford.

- IKEA's senior managers drive themselves to learn not only their own business but their suppliers' businesses as well, so together they can "design the supplier's factory and set up operations" and help lower costs. Again, their chief motivation isn't profit sharing, it's "to create a better everyday life for the majority of people."

SHARED PURPOSE IN OTHER
BUSINESS SUCCESS STORIES

IKEA is just one of many innovative businesses built with a shared purpose.

Take the Disney Company. Walt Disney wasn't trying to "extend the Disney brand" as he battled with lenders and municipalities who thought his Magic Kingdom was a bad bet. Rather, he was driven to create Disneyland by his singular purpose, which was to build a place that *makes people happy*. That purpose, not cold corporate analysis, extended the brand and made for a huge multigenerational success.

Sam Walton wasn't focused on "redefining the paradigm of the twentieth-century supply chain." He persevered through years of difficulties (and there were many tough years for Walton and his executives) so he could build a business where *ordinary folks could buy the same things as rich people*.

Thirty years ago, Charles Schwab sat at a card table planning to do something to better the lives of individual investors. To this day, all 19,000 professionals at his company share that purpose—not to be the biggest or the most profitable, but *to be the world's most ethical and useful financial services firm*.

Michael Cullen didn't see himself or his associates as businesspeople when he wrote his blueprint for creating America's first self-service supermarket. He compared himself to pioneer aviator and national hero Charles Lindbergh, the first man to fly solo across the Atlantic. "Can you imagine how the public would respond to a store of this kind?" Cullen wrote to his then boss, the president of Kroger Markets. "I would be *the miracle man of the grocery business*." Kroger declined to be a part of this purpose, but others joined Cullen to create King Kullen, a revolutionary new idea for grocery retailing.

It's hard to remember now, but back in the early nineties AOL was founded on the purpose *we're going to build a new medium as central to people's lives as the television and the telephone, only more valuable.* That purpose helped Steve Case not only get extraordinary follow-through from employees (especially in the company's treacherous early years) but to engage the assistance of as many as 16,000 volunteers a year (according to *Forbes* magazine, those volunteers, who manned online help centers and monitored chat rooms, saved the company almost $1 billion from 1992 to 2000). Losing sight of that purpose as the company merged with Time Warner certainly contributed to AOL's spectacular decline. According to insiders, it became all about the money at the company instead of providing people with incredibly valuable and convenient technology tools.

George Bernard Shaw explained the attraction of shared purpose for all people. "This is the true joy in life," Shaw wrote, "being used for a purpose recognized by yourself as a mighty one . . . being a force of nature instead of a feverish, selfish little clod of ailments and grievances complaining that the world will not devote itself to making you happy."

FINDING A PURPOSE FOR YOUR TEAM

Not everyone can be in medicine or firefighting, where your work is so obviously connected to a powerful purpose. Nor is every manager a visionary entrepreneur looking to change the world. That makes it difficult for many managers to imagine what their purpose could be.

How mighty can it be to sell shoes, or dinners, or some plants and potting soil? How much purpose can there be in manufacturing power generators, scheduling delivery services, researching pension requirements, or any of the many mundane products and services covered in this book? Can there really be a "shared purpose" that inspires individual initiative in employees in *any* business unit of any size? (Even if you're leading a team in an organization without a purpose?)

Absolutely. There are three places to look:

One, look at what you do through the eyes of your customer.

Two, ask yourself and your people,
"What gets you out of bed in the morning?"

Three, check to see if your motivation could stem from
defeating a common enemy.

THROUGH THE EYES OF THE CUSTOMER

What did you want to be when you grew up? At the age of eight or nine, did you see yourself becoming a businessperson? Or did you instead imagine becoming a veterinarian, a teacher, or a firefighter?

If you listen to kids daydreaming about what they want to be when they become an adult, you'll hear a common theme. The vast majority see themselves doing something that's good for the world.

That's the first place to look for your purpose—the good your products or services do for others. A beautiful garden, the perfect pair of shoes, a pension plan that secures a family's future . . . Inside nearly every product or service (cigarettes and the like excluded), there is the potential to make someone's life significantly better or happier. You just need to look at what you do from the customer's point of view and figure out your purpose by understanding what they love about the products or services you provide.

Seeing your business through the eyes of your customer can have an extraordinary effect on business, as you'll see in this story of a formerly small suburban nursery and its big shared purpose.

CHRIS AND MARIE'S PLANT FARM

Five years ago in Melbourne, Australia, (population about 3.5 million people), there were three small garden centers and a small wholesale nursery called Wombat Gully.

Plant retailing "down under" is just like it is in North America or Europe. There are superstores, local plant shops, and lots of other competition. Margins are low, customers are fickle, and everybody ends up just barely squeezing out a living.

Two partners ran Wombat Gully. Bill, the older of the pair, was a tough, experienced retailer. Bill knew how to run a tight ship— buying plants for less, holding expenses in line, and keeping every employee's nose to the grindstone.

His partner, Chris, was a mad-scientist type. He would taste the soil in a client's garden before prescribing the perfect additives. Chris also would create hybrids, like a tree "you cannot kill." Everything he did was designed to help even "brown thumbs" enjoy their gardens.

One day Chris heard about the power of shared purpose. In a flash, he understood that if he could find his purpose it could inspire everyone in his company to be passionate about their responsibilities.

He looked through the eyes of his customers. "People get incredible joy out of their gardens," Chris explained. "And when I can fill their yard with beauty, especially for less than they thought possible, they're just rapt [that's Aussie for delighted]." So his purpose became *providing the experience of adventure, beauty, and abundance.*

His partner Bill was rather cynical about Chris and this "purpose." He believed business was about making money. Within a few months, the two had irreconcilable differences and decided to part ways.

Have you ever wanted to break up with someone so bad that you didn't care what physical property the other person wanted? That's how Chris felt. So when Bill divided the business—taking the two newest and busiest locations and giving Chris the old corner store miles from the major population areas of Melbourne—Chris didn't care. He wanted the freedom to live his purpose and figured the rest would take care of itself.

In the following three years, Chris went from his position of disadvantage (the worst location, a lot of bills, and plenty of competition) to becoming the most successful plant and garden business, in total sales, of any company in the entire Melbourne marketplace. Not only had he outperformed Bill, he outperformed the bigger, better-resourced superstores. In 2004, Chris and his wife, Marie, opened their fourth location. They have launched an exclusive line

of potting mixes and fertilizers and create dozens of plant innovations, like a tray of fifty annuals that they can sell profitably for
under $10. By the end of 2005, their sales will have grown to ten
times the revenues of the old business, and they may go national (if
Chris can find enough people who want to share his purpose).

Bill has retired.

In today's high-powered world, schlepping plants is as mundane
as the businesses of shoes, pensions, or delivery services. But Chris
saw it as something more because he looked through the eyes of his
customers. And the purpose that his customers' love inspired was a
catalyst for the success of what's now called "Chris and Marie's Plant
Farms." Take a look at what they've done at www.hellohello.com.au.

A REASON THAT GETS YOU OUT OF BED IN THE MORNING

Tom Kelley of IDEO (see the chapter "Create a HOT Team") provided an excellent description of another place to look for your purpose. He said a leader has to provide people with "a reason to get
out of bed in the morning."

A shopping center developer named David explained *his* reason
to get out of bed this way: "This [his project] is the canvas on which
I paint," he said. He got past the aggravation of fighting unreason-
able regulators and the financial risks of speculating on the future
of real estate by focusing on his purpose. This developer saw himself like a painter expressing his artistry by changing the landscape
of communities.

Most managers can figure out what is so fulfilling about their
work that they look forward to getting out of bed to do it. All they
have to do is answer these questions:

1. *What first attracted you to your line of work?*

     A department store vice president remembered what excited
     her most about the prospects of getting her first junior assistant
     buying position. "When I was young, I loved to shop with my
     mother, make new outfits with my grandmother, and get my
     dolls dressed for parties," she said. "My promotion from the sales

floor to the buying office was my chance to dress lots of real women and help them be happier because they looked good."

Something attracted you to your line of work. It just gets lost in the day-to-day grind. Reflect for a moment on the feelings of joy or accomplishment you had when you first got your job. It will put you in touch with what might become a mighty purpose.

2. *What parts of your work life do you use when you are not at work?*

A carpenter stopped at a home center to buy a hinge for a neighbor on his way home from work. Why? He wasn't getting paid. Perhaps it's because he loves the feeling of mastery and is satisfied most when he is helping.

If you can find what you and those around you do at work that makes its way into your free time, you are well on the way to finding a purpose you can share.

3. *If your pay was cut 50 percent but you could cut your work activities by the same amount, what tasks would you keep?*

When asked this question, a family law (divorce) attorney answered, "My job is 15 percent legal expertise and 85 percent guiding clients through the life changes they're about to experience. I know what's coming and I prepare them for it. And they are so much better off, because I keep them from getting stuck in the depths of despair or too caught up in retribution. But if you give me the chance, the one thing I'd get rid of is the 50 percent of my clients who don't appreciate my guidance."

He concluded, "It's just too much work not to get a thank-you!"

Obviously, this professional isn't in it just for the money. His purpose is the satisfaction of appreciation and recognition. What satisfies you so much you'd do it for a reduced salary?

DEFEATING A COMMON ENEMY

Finding a common enemy is another potent source for discovering a shared purpose. After all, one of the most primal human drives is aggression.

An insider at PeopleSoft reported that the merger of JD Edwards and PeopleSoft had been quicker and smoother than anyone expected because for PeopleSoft, looming in the distance was an enemy named Larry Ellison. (In June of 2003, Ellison's company, Oracle, announced a hostile-takeover bid for PeopleSoft.) The folks at PeopleSoft believed Ellison would ruin their way of doing business, which drove them to band together and make the process of merging with JD Edwards go better, showing extraordinary individual initiative.

Health care professionals have experienced the same benefits from their common enemy.

According to a report written by Dr. Jody Hoffer Gittell, "Coordinating Patient Care: A Relational Perspective," "pressures from managed care . . . have begun to reduce some of the obstacles [to better coordination and collaboration at hospitals] by creating an external threat that reduces status boundaries among providers." The phrase "status boundary" means some people think they are better than others—for example, a doctor may act as if his opinion should count more than a nurse's. Now that view has changed, because doctors, nurses, support people, and technicians all have a common enemy, the HMOs.

One doctor explained his new perspective: "We've got a gun to our heads . . . if [we] continue doing things the way we did things, we are going to be a nonentity. . . . It's not a happy place for us." It may not be happy but it has forced doctors and nurses to band together like they never had before.

Michael Harrison used a life-changing event as a common enemy when he started his new company, LightGuard Systems. A buddy of his unintentionally hit a pedestrian. It was a fatal accident. "I saw what this did to him as the motorist," Harrison said, "and how his life was never the same again all because of the design of the crosswalk." So Harrison invented a solution, one that defeated the forces that wreck lives of both pedestrians and drivers. The LightGuard System alerts motorists that they are approaching an occupied crosswalk through flashing amber lights embedded in the roadway and visible up to 1,500 feet.

"I don't know how many lives we've saved, but there are 95,000 injuries and 5,000 deaths annually [when cars fail to stop for pedestrians in crosswalks] and we're doing something about it," Harrison explained. "That purpose helped everyone who works for Light-Guard to put their best efforts into our business despite all the difficulties."

ONCE YOU FIND A PURPOSE, SHARE IT

The story of SSM Health Care (in "More Accurate Assessments") included steps that can be taken to share your purpose.

All 29,000 associates at SSM Health Care are focused on one main mission: *Through our exceptional health care services we reveal the healing presence of God.* It's what gets them out of bed in the morning.

SSM's CEO, Sister Mary Jean Ryan, found this statement of purpose through a process that included the input of more than 3,000 associates. But unlike other companies who have produced similar statements that end up tacked to a wall and are ultimately forgotten, Ryan understood that the purpose (or mission) must be shared.

She started by challenging her executives to write down exactly what their mission committed them to. "Anybody can say they're exceptional," Ryan told them. "We need to define it so we can measure it."

SSM's executives then went out and identified the five factors that together defined an exceptional health care provider: exceptional clinical outcomes; exceptional patient, employee, and physician satisfaction; and exceptional financial results. Then each factor was further defined by benchmarking the industry's performance levels. SSM's senior VP of Strategic Development created the internal measurement systems that would rate member hospitals and every department according to each benchmark.

Next, Ryan and her team worked with each manager on precisely how every associate on their team could contribute to this purpose in their everyday efforts.

Finally, they came up with a scheme for setting employee goals and tracking progress so that each associate could see the results of their efforts and the efforts of everyone else in the system.

Sharing a purpose is more work than simply coming up with an inspirational sentiment. Leaders must:

1. Define the purpose explicitly so it is clear enough to be measured.
2. Communicate the purpose to each employee so they can see how to contribute to living the purpose.
3. Create methods to set goals and measure progress daily, weekly, and monthly—just as you do revenues, costs, and profits.

And to these guidelines add the insight of the FDNY (Fire Department of New York)—find and institutionalize opportunities to *recognize* the contribution of each person who shares your purpose. The FDNY does this, as you'll recall, by having an annual ceremony of remembrance.

OVERCOME CYNICISM AND SKEPTICISM

Leaders looking to use shared purpose to drive individual initiative need to be ready to face a pair of significant obstacles. One is deep-rooted cynicism about the true nature of the capitalist system, and the other is the doubts that have been raised by years of mission and vision exercises and management's lack of follow-through. These are two very different hurdles.

HOW TO HANDLE THE CYNICS

Like Bill (Chris's original partner in the nursery business), many believe that business is built solely on self-interest; that a person's desire to get more for themselves—to fatten their wallets and improve their material welfare—drives their initiative and nothing more. "This is a job and that's all there is to it. . . . we work our butts off just to put food on the table," says the wage earner. "It's a dog-eat-dog world out there," harrumphs a hard-nosed executive. "There's no time for a lot of mush about values and purpose."

Author Dinesh D'Souza spoke to this point of view in his article in the now-defunct *Industry Standard.* "Let's not kid ourselves," he wrote in "Looking for Meaning in All the WRONG Places," "what work is really for . . . is to make stuff and make money." In other words, suggesting that managers need to worry as much about a higher purpose as intensely as they do about hitting budget is putting spiritual principles in the wrong place.

That conclusion is remarkably similar to the cynical reaction Henry Ford heard in 1914 when he decided to double the pay of his workforce.

"The most foolish thing ever attempted," said industrialists. The publisher of the *New York Times* remarked, "He's crazy, isn't he?" And the voice of capitalism, the *Wall Street Journal,* criticized Ford's decision as "the application of spiritual principles where they don't belong."

Perhaps because of those criticisms, years later Ford made it sound like his true motivation for this pay raise was to cut costs (by reducing worker turnover) and drive up demand (by creating a whole new group of consumers who could afford the cars Ford made). But those were a pair of good but unintended consequences, according to Ford biographer Robert Lacey.

Lacey concludes that the automaker would have never changed his pay plan had it not been for what Ralph Waldo Emerson wrote about the purposes behind wages. "He is great who confers the most benefits," Emerson wrote in his essay "Compensation." "He is base . . . to receive favors and render none. Beware of too much good staying in your hand." Realizing all the money he was saving with his new methods of manufacturing and taking Emerson's words into account, Ford decided to share the wealth in a spirit of "true generosity," Lacey wrote.

The first step in dealing with deep-rooted cynicism as a force against purpose is to be resolute that spiritual principles *do* have a place in business decisions. Near the opening of this chapter, read the stories of entrepreneurs (like Ingvar Kamprad of IKEA) who achieved their greatest successes by having a purpose. Settle on the fact that this is a core belief for you and that no cynic is going to shake your resolve.

The second step is to realize that there's no place in your purpose-driven team for leaders who don't share that belief. Many business-people are too embittered, too caught up in self-interest, or perhaps just too pragmatic (they think) to let purpose, honor, contribution, and passion motivate them. That's fine. Leave it as merely a matter of personal outlook. But invite these cynics to find another team. Chris (from Chris and Marie's Plant Farm) did, and it worked out fine for both Chris and Bill.

SKEPTICISM VERSUS CYNICISM

Don't confuse deep-rooted cynicism with a sensible skepticism. The concept of finding a purpose you can share in your work has been tried before. In the seventies it was called a mission statement, and in the eighties a vision. But whatever it was called, usually no one ever followed through. In thousands of companies, these statements were put on the wall and added to the in-house communications. But they were never really shared among employees in an effective way or made a real business priority.

Many managers expected having a shared purpose would work as it did in Shakespeare's *Henry IV*. They wanted someone to make a speech and then expected that instantly all the troops would rally. But that's not the way it happens in the real world.

"The first time [your people hear about your purpose], they're not really paying attention," said Bill Zollars, the CEO of Yellow Roadway Corporation. "They're sitting and wondering, 'How long is this guy (or gal) going to last?' and 'How can we work around what they're saying until they move on?'"

Zollars spent a year and a half traveling to every office and conducting town hall meetings to share his purpose: *Stop thinking of yourself as a trucking company, start thinking like a service provider.* His advice to anyone on a similar mission—don't be impatient.

"It [their reaction] starts with blank stares . . . maybe 10 percent of the people are nodding." But, Zollars continued, "By the second or third time maybe it's 40 percent who are nodding. By then you've got some evidence. . . . You've got your stories and some facts they can relate to. And some stuff they can use to check your credibility. And that's when it takes off.

"You have to go back to the same place three or four times and say the same thing," Zollars said. "We kept putting it up in front of them, saying [in essence] this is why we were talking about this stuff [and] this is why it's important. And not only was I saying it, but all the other members of the management team were saying it. We were just absolutely relentless about the message."

Zollars learned that you will win over the skeptics only with consistent shows of commitment. Don't plan to share your purpose until you're sure you're ready to follow through on it relentlessly.

12 SHOW MORE RESPECT

■

Just before midnight on May 9, 1996, a Manhattan socialite, a Dallas doctor, a Seattle postal worker, and nineteen other extreme adventurers left Base Camp IV for the peak of Mount Everest. Their expedition was led by a pair of well-respected high-altitude mountaineers working for two world-renowned companies, Rob Hall from Adventure Consultants and Scott Fischer from Mountain Madness.

The plan was to reach the summit by midday and have everybody back in their tents before dark. But things didn't go as planned. In spite of Scott Fischer's rule—*if you're not to the top by two, it's time to turn around*—seventeen of the twenty-two climbers, including Fischer and Hall, continued toward the peak well past 2 P.M. True to the worry that inspired Fischer's edict, the late-afternoon descent was a disaster. Signals got crossed, bottlenecks caused further delays, and the oxygen ran out. When a blizzard with hurricane-force gusts unexpectedly hammered the expedition, the amateurs and their guides both became disoriented. Out of twenty-two climbers, five died, including Hall and Fischer. The others were either seriously injured or severely traumatized.

The story of that awful adventure has been told many times. It inspired a best-selling book, journalist Jon Krakauer's *Into Thin Air*, and numerous magazine articles and a made-for-TV movie. But there's an important lesson buried deep in that harrowing experience that's gone mostly unnoticed—a message every manager needs to understand about the vital link between respect and her team's initiative, especially in volatile situations where time is short and the stakes are high.

THE LESSON FROM EVEREST

Accidents and deaths are not isolated incidents on Mount Everest. Over the years, 160 mountaineers have been lost trying to reach the peak.

Because of those risks, Hall and Fischer made it clear to their amateur adventurers that they should adhere to a strict client/guide protocol. "We were specifically indoctrinated not to question our guides' judgment," Krakauer wrote in *Into Thin Air*.

According to Krakauer, Rob Hall made sure everybody understood the gravity of this protocol by issuing a strict directive. "I will tolerate no dissension up there," he said to everyone in camp. "My word will be absolute law, beyond appeal. If you don't like a particular decision I make, I'd be happy to discuss it with you afterward, not while we're up on the hill."

Hall was like a lot of managers who give their people precise commands and demand unconditional obedience. He was worried about two things: (a) keeping missteps to a minimum and (b) getting everything done on schedule.

Hall was concerned that should something disrupt the expedition's tight schedule, his less-experienced teammates might be so committed to "bagging the top" (continuing to climb even when told it was not safe to keep on going) that they would argue with him instead of respecting his instructions. He was also concerned about safety. These people were, after all, his responsibility, and he didn't want them to make a bad decision and injure themselves or someone else.

But despite these good intentions, his strict directives and demands for absolute compliance must have left the climbers feeling as if Hall didn't respect them. If you read between the lines of Hall's client/guide protocol, you can see how that impression could have been made.

Any amateur on Mount Everest starts out with feelings of great vulnerability. They're alone among strangers, in a hostile environment, facing dangers beyond anything they've ever experienced. To minimize these feelings of vulnerability, each climber had spent a lot of money (as much as $65,000) to hire an expert like Hall to *look out for them*.

Now, on the mountain, this trusted guide tells them, "If you don't *like* a particular decision I make, I'd be happy to discuss it with you afterward, not while we're up on the hill." Note that Hall's use of the word *like* is an emotionally charged choice that implies immaturity and even pettiness. The idea that there could be any oversight in the expert's thinking or any complication that the leader failed to recognize is totally rejected by the choice of words and the tone of the directive. This command implies that the man hired to assure the best outcomes doesn't trust the team's thinking. In fact, the message goes one step further, saying, in effect, the client shouldn't trust his or her own judgment.

Read between the lines and you'll see another strong admonition. By stating, "I will tolerate no dissension up there," the leader in effect has labeled anyone who does speak up a dissenter. *Dissent* is another emotionally loaded word, especially in team-based activities. Dissent suggests that someone might be being selfish, egotistical, and overall a bad teammate. The underlying message is clear—to be considered a good colleague, clients should do what they're told and keep quiet.

How could anyone keep their good opinion of themselves after all that?

A LACK OF RESPECT LEADS TO A LACK OF INITIATIVE

Brandeis professor Jody Hoffer Gittell, author of *The Southwest Airlines Way: Using the Power of Relationships to Achieve High*

Performance, has studied the relationship between respect and effective follow-through in high-stakes situations like the ones hospitals and airlines face every day. Her research connects a lack of respect with a lack of initiative.

"Respect . . . encourages participants to consider the impact of actions on others, reinforcing their inclination to coordinate," she explains. And "respect [also] increases the problem-solving nature of communications." Both are critical to the initiative required for following through.

Failure to consider the effect of one's actions on others and a lack of solution-oriented communication clearly had a role in what happened during that disastrous Everest descent:

- Doug Hansen (one of the clients) had been on Everest with Hall in 1995. Unfortunately, during that climb Hall turned Hansen around just 330 vertical feet from the top. This time Hansen said, "I've put too much of myself into this mountain to quit." As two o'clock passed, Hansen was still far from the top. Yet Hall did not stop him. Teammates recognized that Hall was breaking the two-o'clock rule, endangering himself and Hansen, but no one spoke up.

- Logistical snafus and a recurrence of an old illness impaired Scott Fischer's physical condition. He lagged far behind his team and was laboring hard to reach the summit. Team members noticed that Fischer continued to climb long after his deadline, but again they kept their concerns to themselves.

- Andy Harris was one of the group's "invincible" guides. Unfortunately, blizzard conditions caused his oxygen gauge to malfunction. So when he told the team that the oxygen canisters at the South Summit were all empty, he was mistaken. No one questioned him or even considered the possibility that Harris might be wrong, according to Krakauer. The result was that life-saving oxygen went unused.

- A lack of initiative affected the guides as well as the amateurs. According to Krakauer, when guide Neil Beidleman saw Fischer and others continuing well past midday, he was uncomfortable telling his boss to follow his own rule and turn around. "I tried not to be too pushy," Beidleman said. "I didn't always speak up when maybe I should have, and now I kick myself for it." Anatoli Boukreev, another member of the leadership, was concerned about certain team members' fitness levels. But Boukreev also stayed quiet. "I tried not to be argumentative, choosing instead to downplay my intuitions," he said.

As you can see from these examples, the problem with strict directives and demands for absolute compliance is that they remove a critical safety valve that protects the group when the leaders are wrong.

In his article "Lessons from Everest," Professor Michael Roberto of Harvard wrote how the loss of respect affected the outcomes that day. "Effective teams discuss issues and encourage members to present dissenting views. These behaviors help to combat miscalculations and misjudgments. At critical junctures [Hall's and Fischer's] teams did not discuss mistakes openly, exchange information freely, and challenge prevailing views and assumptions." As a result, Roberto concludes, "it [was] difficult to identify and solve problems before they trigger[ed] a series of other breakdowns."*

Dr. Gittell connects Roberto's lesson from Everest to everyday business. "When tasks are interdependent, circumstances are unpredictable, and time is of the essence, *respect is critical*," Gittell teaches. "Real or perceived, a lack of respect threatens a business's push for greater quality and more efficient outcomes."

FROM EVEREST TO EVERYDAY BUSINESS

Most managers struggle to show enough respect. It isn't because they are cold or rude by nature. It's just that when management finds itself in volatile, fast-changing situations where the priorities are (a) keeping missteps to a minimum and (b) getting to the objective on schedule, they fall back on the same leadership tactics that failed on Everest—giving people strict directives and demanding absolute compliance.

*Michael A. Roberto, "Lessons from Everest," *California Management Review*, Vol. 45, No. 1, Fall 2002.

Michael Maybrun saw this happen in his career.

"For years I worked to refine the business of home electronics retailing," Maybrun, an entrepreneur, remembered. "I had collected a lot of the pieces. I had a system for purchasing, merchandising, staff management, and customer service that were reliable, practical, and profitable."

Then Maybrun met someone who could provide better retail marketing and promotions—the only two holes in his business model. When the two put their heads together they had, as Scott Fischer said of his plan to scale Everest, "a yellow brick road to the summit."

Early results reinforced Maybrun's confidence. Everything he and his new associate implemented worked out incredibly well. "Within ninety days, we started doubling our revenues," Maybrun recalls. "That got everybody really excited. Salespeople were selling a lot more, we started expanding and creating more opportunities for advancement at every level. The buzz was really positive. Our suppliers told the industry we had perfected a new business model for the fast-changing world of consumer electronics. Competitors started copying us. We felt invincible."

That feeling of invincibility led the pair to insist on absolute compliance from their organization, just as Hall and Fischer did on Everest. "We decided the best way to keep any missteps to a minimum and get to our goals fast was to insist everyone follow though without deviation," Maybrun said.

So the pair installed an intensive training system that emphasized the *one right way* to do everything. They backed the training up with a strict accountability system that assured everybody moved in lockstep.

But as on Everest, the pair's good intentions resulted in several negative consequences:

- **Everybody was made to feel uncomfortable with expressing dissent.** "If we let every decision turn into a debate or let people question our direction at every turn, it's going to slow us down," Maybrun's associate told him. "I don't think we need any help in

figuring things out." Dissenters were given the unspoken message that they were probably too lazy, too uncommitted, or too
undisciplined to be worthy of being a part of such a high-caliber
organization.

- **Everybody's self-respect was put at risk.** People are motivated
  by respect. They'll do a lot to get it. Maybrun's associate was
  a master at using people's need for respect to get them to work
  harder. "They became so afraid of doing anything that would
  cost them his good opinion," Maybrun admits. "They put their
  heads down and followed through as instructed. Their fear of
  losing his respect kept the staff from thinking for themselves."
- **Deference was the unspoken standard.** "He was a good soldier," Maybrun said of his associate. "He had a great appreciation for my role in building that business. Consequently, out of
  respect, he would always defer to me whenever I felt strongly
  about something—even though sometimes his own best judgment was guiding him in a different direction. And then he
  would work really hard to make my opinions or initiatives pre-
  vail. The result was that [the maxim] *my leader right or wrong*
  became part of the unspoken company culture."

That all worked fine for about six years. Then, just like on Everest, lots of little things started to go wrong and the lack of respect
throughout the company compounded its problems.

"We started missing margin budget and the sales budget due to
a recession," Maybrun said. "At the same time, a competitor
recruited several key associates. Revenues slid still further while we
tried to get new people up to speed. When one store was shut down
for a week during the earthquake, profits evaporated. By then
nobody in leadership was thinking clearly. Our only reaction was to
issue more directives and demand even stricter compliance. That
led to more key defections, more missed budgets, and more losses.
Before I knew it, it was chaos. Everybody got disoriented just trying
to survive."

But it was too late. After two more years of thrashing around,
Maybrun closed the doors on his once high-flying business.

"Looking back, we could have made it through the recession and the earthquake," Maybrun concluded. But an unwillingness of the rank and file to take initiative and a lack of communications made everything that much worse.

"The signs were there to be seen well in advance," Maybrun explained. "The sales staff saw it was getting harder and harder to win deals. They recognized customers didn't value our value-added services as much as they had just two years earlier. It was nearly impossible for our buyers to get the same manufacturer support we had the year before. Office staff heard the complaints of defectors long before the rift was beyond repair. But nobody said anything, or if they did they couldn't get through," Maybrun explained.

"Had I understood the role respect can play in making sure leaders take the right steps to keep problems from becoming a disaster," Maybrun said, "I would have made it one of our top priorities."

MORE RESPECT CREATES MORE INITIATIVE

Joan Beglinger works in another volatile, fast-changing industry where any mistake or misstep can be as dangerous as a wrong move on Everest. Beglinger is the vice president of Patient Services for St. Marys Hospital, a big facility in downtown Madison, Wisconsin, that provides all the acute-care services—emergency room, cardiac care, infant intensive care, and neuroscience—as well as primary care in orthopedics, obstetrics, and geriatrics.

For years Beglinger managed her hospital much like the expedition on Everest. "I started out thinking that as the vice president I was responsible for controlling all the outcomes at St. Marys Hospital," Beglinger said. She viewed her priorities just as the Everest experts and Maybrun viewed theirs: (a) keep missteps to a minimum and (b) meet every objective on schedule. She followed the same leadership model—generating strict directives and requiring compliance. "It was awesome, it kept me awake at nights," Beglinger admitted, and explained, "I believed that to control all the outcomes, I had to control all the people and all their decisions."

St. Marys' outcomes were fine, but still about average for the industry. Beglinger wanted to be better. That dissatisfaction led her to have a flash of insight.

"We [the executives and directors] can't control the outcomes," she realized late one night. "Management *can* write a policy that says, 'Under normal conditions this is what we do.' But in a hospital, someone has to decide, 'Is there anything [not normal] about this particular situation? Is there *some* reason that would cause us to think about it differently?' That on-the-spot judgment call is critical to achieving good outcomes in health care. I can't make that decision. No executive can. It's made at the bedside."

That conclusion led Beglinger to stop all managers from issuing strict directives and demanding unquestioned compliance. "I don't try to control the outcomes anymore. That puts too much of the burden on me to be right all the time," she said. "I can only support those who provide care at the point of service so they manage the outcomes effectively."

Beglinger altered her hospital's leadership perspective from a traditional command-and-control mind-set to one of "shared governance." Shared governance is just what it sounds like—nine hundred nurses and nursing staff working with financial and systems managers together to decide how the hospital will run. "We rely on one another—not a hierarchy—to improve the environment in which we work and the patient care that we provide," Beglinger said. "As a team, we make decisions that shape the culture and success of the nursing organization. *Each nurse has a voice in those decisions.*"

The client/guide protocol of that disastrous Everest expedition and Maybrun's "one right way" to do everything are the polar opposite of the concept of shared governance. Those leaders thought the best way to assure good decisions and desired outcomes was to *limit* the participation of the team. They told their associates in many implicit and explicit ways that their input wasn't valuable. As Maybrun said, "I believed we had been there and done that. We [the two at the top] were best qualified to call the shots."

The practice of shared governance runs in the other direction, in the process creating a powerful show of respect. As the leaders at St.

Marys increased the participation of every level of employee, they in effect told associates that not only was everyone's input valuable, it was *superior* to the judgment of the executives working alone. So in one burst of inspiration Beglinger reversed the practices that cut into everyone's good opinion of themselves.

The effect of Beglinger's changes in management is apparent in the group's collaboration, problem-solving, and initiative efforts.

- Collaboration. "All the units help each other," St. Marys unit Secretary Lynn Crabtree explained. "We ask, 'How can *we* give the best patient care and how can *we* be good to the families?'"

    Nurse Wendy Wittner confirmed Crabtree's assessment: "I feel like we're all in this together, from the VPs to the housekeepers."

- Problem solving. Intensive Care nurse Larry Dauffenbach commented on the increase in communication at St. Marys: "If something's not being done, it's our responsibility to make sure corrective action is taken. Here, it's everybody helping each other and trying to make everybody better."

    "I used to blame other people for the way things were," Surgical nurse Karen Brennan noted. "Now [I know that] the patient care is only going to improve if *I* work on it."

- Initiative. "At first it is kind of a scary concept to have all this responsibility," said Eunice Simmons, director of Intensive Care. "But now *I know* I can make that decision, and I do."

    "St. Marys encourages and expects us all to grow," according to Barb Oswald from Ambulatory Surgery. "You just don't realize all the leadership capabilities you have."

SHOWING MORE RESPECT EQUALS
SHOWING MORE PROFITS

Respect has saved St. Marys money that other hospitals budget as an expected cost of doing business.

"Our turnover rates are less than half the national average [9 versus 21 percent]," Beglinger noted.

One industry estimate concluded that each new nursing hire costs about $11,000 to recruit and as much as $74,000 in lost productivity during the hiring and training process. If a hospital like

St. Marys with 900 nurses has a 21 percent turnover rate (the national average), the direct out-of-pocket expenses would be almost $2 million a year, with indirect costs of over $13 million. Half the turnover would save half that money.

St. Marys also has a full-time staff vacancy rate of just 3 percent, a fraction of the national average of 19 percent. This also saves money and makes for higher patient revenues.

Vacancy means a hospital has the need for more nurses than they are able to find. Depending on the department, a hospital needs one skilled nurse for every two to six patients, so when a hospital has a 19 percent vacancy rate, as many do, it cuts into revenues deeply. Vacancy also adds to the hospital budget for temporary agency nurses ($28 million at one health care system last year) and lowers the quality of care. Studies show a direct connection between the ratio of nurses to patients and mortality—the fewer the full-time nurses, the higher the rate.

"We've got the answer to the nursing shortage," Beglinger said flatly. "Nurses aren't willing to work as hard as they do and leave every day feeling bad." Showing them more respect makes them feel better about what they do and, in the process, leads to higher retention and lower vacancy rates.

Additionally, according to William Thompson, the Senior Vice President of Strategic Development for the health care group that owns St. Marys, "In the areas of patient satisfaction/loyalty, operating margin, and physician satisfaction as well as employee satisfaction, St. Marys ranks either at the top or near the top of all [twenty] hospitals in our group." Considering that his group is the 2002 Baldrige National Award for Quality winner, that's high praise. "Their program [of shared governance] is the reason they do so well, even among some of the best in their class," said Thompson.

HOW TO SHOW MORE RESPECT

Every business isn't ready for the radical changes required to implement Beglinger's system of shared governance. It took her years to get all the councils and the processes up and running. But that doesn't mean they can't make the major strides Beglinger made in showing more respect. She offers two suggestions for doing so: First, all managers should check their assumptions, and second, every manager should make it a priority to nurture the staff's self-confidence.

FIRST: CHECK YOUR ASSUMPTIONS

In 1989, a British Midlands 737 was flying shuttle service from London to Belfast. Shortly after takeoff, the cockpit crew heard a loud bang, felt the plane shudder, and began to smell burning metal.

According to the instrument panel, the problem was in the right engine. The pilot immediately began shutting that engine down.

What the pilot didn't know was something every passenger on the left side could see. The left engine was the one throwing off sparks and smoke. The right engine was fine.

Just as the pilot finished shutting the right engine down, the left engine failed. Forty-seven people died.

Beglinger would say mental models blinded that pilot, as it never occurred to him to check what his gauges said and consult with people who had less or no expertise.

Mental models are another term for assumptions. Beglinger believes it's management's assumptions that lead them to make decisions and take actions that damage employee confidence. "Our mental models underestimate our staff and rob the organization of their potential," she said.

The amount of trust you show your people is critical to their self-esteem. But your decision to trust them usually is founded not on facts but rather on assumptions you have about the very nature of working people. Check yours out with the quiz below:

	Yes	No
Do you believe most people are trustworthy?	❏	❏
Do you believe most people welcome responsibility?	❏	❏
Do you believe most people prefer work to being idle?	❏	❏
Do you believe most people seek meaning from their work?	❏	❏

Do you believe most people want to learn?   ❏   ❏
Do you believe most people won't resist change if
   it's handled right?   ❏   ❏

Your answers will reveal your mental model of your associate's mind-set. That model influences how you communicate, the priorities you set, and how you interpret the feedback you get from employees for every action you take. Managers who answer "yes" to the questions in the quiz will see the same event differently than those who answer "no."

To show more respect, you don't need to take a class in building self-esteem in others or use a handbook of encouraging words. You just need to examine your assumptions and decide if they're causing you to view the world in a way that hurts your organization's self-respect.

Beglinger looked at three mental models common in the workforce and altered each in her own mind with the goal of showing more respect to her associates.

• **Assumption**—*Only the bosses need to know the financial details.*

"When I came here, the front-line managers did not see all the budgets," Beglinger explained. "The thinking was if we share that information, they [the staff] will learn we are a very profitable hospital, get disgruntled, and want more money or stop being worried about the costs." Beglinger thought this assumption showed a lack of respect, underestimating the staff's maturity. "If we understand the value of generating a healthy margin, why can't they?" she asked.

"Why can't I tell them about the $110-million addition we need and say, 'If we don't operate at a profit, we can't make the investment'? If they understand everything we're thinking and everything we know, they are more likely to be totally invested, because it will make sense to them."

So today everybody at St. Marys sees the monthly income statement (translated for nonaccountants). They know everything the bosses know—including all the finances.

- **Assumption**—*If they don't get it, it's because they're not ready to get it.*

"When we first began our program of shared decision making, I thought, 'If we just give nurses freedom, you know, turn them loose, everything will get better in a hurry,'" Beglinger explained. "But we found out fast that they don't necessarily know how [to handle things without direction]."

Beglinger turned the teacher/student mental model on its head. Most managers wonder why they can't find smart people who "get" what they are trying to say. But Beglinger says if they aren't getting it, it's because the managers need to better their skills as teachers and coaches. That subtle shift makes a big difference in how much respect a team feels they are getting from their managers.

"We had to do more than create a structure where they [have the freedom to] share in the decision," Beglinger explained. "We had to give them the information and teach them how to take charge and make good decisions. Now the burden is on us [the top executives]. We have to answer the question 'Are we good at teaching?' rather than asking ourselves 'Are they smart enough to get it?' "

In the process of examining this assumption, Beglinger learned, "People want to do what they do well. They want to learn, they want to develop, they want to play a part in something important."

- **Assumption**—*Those at the top know best.*

Initially, Beglinger said, "We couldn't imagine employees at the staff levels sharing [the] important decisions about direction." This mental model was based on the assumption that the boss knows more than everyone else.

Beglinger was trained as a clinical nurse specialist, an advanced-practice professional who's managed many kinds of health care situations. To this day, she puts on scrubs one full day a month and works shoulder to shoulder with the nurses at the patient's bedside. So she's far from being a disconnected, ivory-tower executive. But when she sits on one of the governing councils, she sits alongside staffers from the front lines as a fellow member. "I have influence," Beglinger said, "but *no* veto power."

"Look, I may be at the bedside one day a month and I may have more experience [than nurses at the front lines]," she said, "but I'm not clinically competent. I can't go out and take care of patients; I don't even recognize the drugs. I've been away too long. You've got to be a current practitioner to have real expertise in our profession." And *real* expertise is what adds the most value to a hospital's decision making.

Can you imagine a vice president in your organization suggesting they lacked the necessary expertise to form an opinion or veto something some staff person decided? No, usually their ego would get in the way.

"They're not evil powermongers," Beglinger added. "I know. I was concerned when I first decided to share governance. I liked being in charge. But I am today more powerful than I ever imagined, because I am the VP of an organization that is humming along with all these talented people producing so much. . . . It doesn't detract from me."

Now at St. Marys, they respect the opinions of those who do the work, giving them the power to make critical decisions.

SECOND: NURTURE THEIR CONFIDENCE

The second part of Beglinger's prescription for showing more respect is to nurture the staff's confidence. "If we want people to make their best decisions given the circumstances they face, then the way we deal with them when mistakes are made, or things don't go the way we imagined they would, determines whether or not they will be willing to risk using their judgment," she said.

• *Encourage disagreements.*

Imagine you and your boss have a difference of opinion and your boss says, "Do what you think best." If it turns out you're right, will your boss say anything? On the other hand, if you're wrong and your boss had the better way, will you hear about it? Beglinger believes the way a boss deals with staff decision making is crucial, especially when employees choose a different course than the boss suggests.

"Rarely does anything get done exactly as I would decide to do it," Beglinger said. "So I've trained myself to look for situations where it works out better because they *didn't* go in my direction. I say, 'Well, I was definitely wrong on that one!'" This reinforces their feeling of comfort and safety about following their own instincts. It nurtures the team's confidence.

Some managers let the staff follow their own path but then hover over every step with a frown. The moment something isn't going as planned, they swoop in to save the day. They think they are being protective and supportive, but actually they are cutting into the team member's self-esteem. It's like having an overprotective mother.

"One of my measures of progress is when I offer my opinion and the others say, 'Thank you very much, but we're going to go in a different direction,'" Beglinger said. "That tells me we're in a good place. If people always go in my direction, that puts too much pressure on me to always be right."

- *Check what you do when things don't go as planned.*

Beglinger believes leaders have to create an atmosphere in which they support their people and demonstrate that support unequivocally when the chips are down. The story of a medical malpractice suit illustrates the extent to which she's made nurturing the staff's confidence a priority.

> During a psychiatric examination the patient went from being cooperative and well-controlled to an extremely agitated state without warning. He jumped from the floor to a bed and off the bed into a wall. He hit the wall with so much force, he broke his neck and was paralyzed.
>
> St. Marys was sued for malpractice.
>
> Beglinger sat there in the courtroom every day of the trial with the nurses who were on duty. "I sat [with them] until 4 A.M. the night of the verdict," she said.
>
> "I knew those nurses. The outcome was awful, but their practice was sound," Beglinger explained.

She also knew the whole organization was wondering what was going to happen if St. Marys lost that megamillion-dollar lawsuit. But those nurses continued to practice at St. Marys.

Beglinger's actions showed everyone on staff that they would not be "hung out to dry" when bad things happened, as they inevitably will.

When it comes to nurturing confidence, commitment, and constructive dissent among your team, Beglinger believes it's not what you say but what you do that makes the difference. Under her leadership, all nine hundred nurses and staff know she is behind them even when the chips are down.

Many companies send the opposite signal. Consider the case of an incident at a bank in California:

Ben, a regional bank executive, stopped at a local office while traveling to use their computer. He sat down at an open desk near the back and started working.

Without warning, a disturbed customer walked up and threw a punch at him. Ben instinctively reacted, deflecting the blow, grabbing the customer by the shirt, and planting the customer's face down on the desk.

Security guards saw the scuffle and rushed over to hold on to the disturbed customer and call the police. As they were waiting, the assailant broke free and ran out of the building.

Two weeks after the incident, the customer filed a lawsuit against the bank. In his investigation, the bank's senior manager asked Ben, "What did you do to provoke this customer?"

Ben had done nothing.

To Ben this executive was assuming the worst of a colleague and the best of a deranged customer. Ben didn't feel supported or respected. In fact, he felt the opposite.

When an opportunity to join another bank came along, Ben took it.

Business is unanimous. Everyone wants their people to behave like partners looking to solve problems before they turn into disasters and to consider the effect of their actions on the overall good of the organization. These are two critical components of what we think of as individual initiative. But the lesson from Everest, along with the other examples in this chapter, is that unless you show your people respect they won't show you that kind of initiative.

Examine how you give directives, how you make decisions, what you do when things don't go as planned, and what those actions say to your people. Make showing more respect a priority.

13 FIND THE LINE BETWEEN ENOUGH AND TOO MUCH ACCOUNTABILITY

■

I t's hard to imagine that there's such a thing as *too much* account-ability.

Twenty years ago, Ed Locke of the University of Maryland stud-ied four of the most popular management tactics for producing bet-ter outcomes. Locke and his colleagues concluded that setting accountable goals was far and away the most powerful strategy a manager could implement, improving performance an average of 16 percent.*

A decade later, research from McKinsey and Company recon-firmed the value of accountability. Comparing the factors that sep-arated high-performing units from mediocre ones, consultants Katzenbach and Smith concluded that giving teams challenging and meaningful goals and letting them know how they were doing was the *one* distinguishing factor when separating the best-performing teams from the rest.[†]

*Rynes, Brown, and Colbert, "Seven Common Misconceptions About Human Resource Practices," *Academy of Management Executive*, Vol. 18, No. 3, 2002.
[†]Ibid.

Accountability is inescapably linked to following through. In "Clear Expectations," we learned that leaders must start by dividing their big goals into pieces, then designate who's responsible for each. Later, they follow up to see if things are going well and, if not, decide what intervention is necessary. Accountability is the only way those in charge can know who owns each part of an overall goal and decide if they are following through.

So it's hard to imagine that a business could have *too much* accountability. According to research, it is the single most effective tactic for improving individual and team performance and an integral part of the formula for keeping things from falling through the cracks.

Yet new studies conclude that managers have to be careful about how much accountability they impose.

"Systems of accountability and performance measurement, rather than being ideal . . . have unintended negative consequences," writes author and researcher Dr. Jody Hoffer Gittell, a faculty member in the MIT Global Airline Industry program. Gittell studied the application of accountability in organizations for her article in the *California Management Review,* "Paradox of Coordination and Control." She discovered that managers who take accountability too far, especially in businesses where follow-through requires rapid responses to unpredictable changes, chip away at each individual's willingness to look past personal interests and work with others to make sure what's expected gets done.

In other words, she identified a point where the process of setting individual goals and measuring performance stops adding value and actually undermines initiative.

Where is the line that divides *enough* from *too much* accountability? Is it the same in every business and for every manager? And how can leaders decide in advance how much accountability will be too much?

To get these questions answered, let's first reconfirm just what is meant by "accountability" in an ideal world. Then we'll look inside a less-than-ideal workplace and see what happened when they pushed total accountability too far. Last, we'll list three assessments you must make before you decide how much accountability is too much.

ACCOUNTABILITY IN AN IDEAL WORLD

What's your reaction when someone says "You're accountable"? Some people get stressed at the mere mention of those two words.

A search of *Roget's Interactive Thesaurus* explains why. The site lists *answerable*, *culpable*, *liable*, and *on the hook* as synonyms. No wonder the phrase "You're accountable" makes people uptight. They connect it to getting called on the carpet or being made a scapegoat.

But according to Spencer Johnson and Ken Blanchard's *The One Minute Manager*—the 1981 bestseller that introduced accountability to more than ten million readers—accountability is not about designating someone to blame.

Blanchard and Johnson tell the story of a young businessperson out to find the most highly effective management tactics—and the highly effective manager who could teach them to him. The seeker met with many types of leaders from the four corners of the globe (according to the authors). All those leaders fell into one of two camps—"tough" managers who focused on business results to the detriment of their people, or "nice" managers focused on people to the detriment of their business results. Wasn't there a way for leaders to run their units, this young man wondered, "so that both the people and the organization profit from their presence?"

Then he met the world's most effective businessperson, who told him there was indeed a way. According to the mythical "One Minute Manager," to run a business so that both the people and the organization do well, a manager needs to master accountability— by setting one minute goals with every subordinate and then following up with what the book called "one minute praisings" and "one minute reprimands." In the world of the One Minute Manager, accountability had nothing to do with designating who's on the hook. Accountability was a partnership, where smart, creative, and hardworking managers turned big expectations into clearly understood pieces, mutually agreed with some individual or group that they should take responsibility for their part, and then followed up with useful and constructive feedback.

When you look at accountability from the One Minute Manager's perspective, it seems to be an ideal solution for both managers and employees. As one manager told Dr. Gittell, "People are naturally competitive. They absolutely need to know the score. Once they know, they will do something about it."* Ideally, accountability gives everyone their score and compels each individual to do the right thing.

Which leads us back to the original question: How could such a logical and humane practice ever go too far?

The answer is it can't—in a fictional, idealized workplace. But if you consider those critical adverbs and adjectives—*clearly* understood pieces, *mutually* agreed responsibilities, and *useful* constructive feedback—and then watch the practice in real life, where situations are complex, time is short, and every participant is different, you can imagine how easy it is for managers to cross the line and have too much accountability undermine an individual's or group's initiative.

THE REAL WORLD OF AMERICAN AIRLINES

It was two years after the Carter administration deregulated the airline industry that Robert Crandall was first named the president of American Airlines. Crandall was worried that the end of government controls would cause his competitors to begin discounting their services in order to gain market share. In his mind, any knee-jerk price wars would be a major threat to his airline's bottom line.

So Crandall decided to take preemptive action, to change his business faster on the inside than others would change things on the outside. He invented a hub-and-spoke system for airline scheduling, giving American a 20 percent revenue advantage over his competitor's point-to-point systems. He dreamed up frequent-flyer awards to lock passengers into flying on his airline. And Crandall originated the use of supercomputers for passenger forecasting, giv-

*Dr. Jody Hoffer Gittell, "Paradox of Coordination and Control," *California Management Review*, Vol. 42, No. 3.

ing American the ability to be more responsive and more productive than all other carriers.

Each innovation was very successful accomplishing just what Crandall intended. In twelve years, American's new president tripled sales (from $6 to $18 billion) and led his industry in profits. Many of his competitors went bankrupt.

Crandall didn't stop with technical and marketing innovations. He was also one of the first big-company CEOs to realize that a *deregulated* business needed to keep demanding and informed customers from defecting. That meant they had to do everything in their power to avoid frustrating the traveling public (as any dissatisfaction is a catalyst for customer defection). So he proposed another big innovation: total front-line accountability for avoiding customer disappointment.

THE GOAL—MORE ON-TIME DEPARTURES

Customers expect a lot of things from their air carrier. Right at the top of the list (after safety) is flights that take off on time and baggage that shows up at the destination, also on time. If either of these elementary expectations is not met, the customer is very disappointed.

When you are sitting in the departure lounge, an on-time departure and correct baggage handling seems like a pretty simple request. But like everything that seems so simple to customers of your business, getting a plane off on time is much more difficult than it looks.

Each departure is the result of a long list of activities, performed in sequence, under changing circumstances, in a very limited amount of time, by *twelve* different functional groups of employees: ticket agents, gate agents, pilots, flight attendants, cabin cleaners, caterers, baggage handlers, ramp agents, mechanics, fuelers, operations agents, and freight handlers.

American's hub-and-spoke system added complications to this complex process. Hub-and-spoke means regional passengers fly into a central hub (like Chicago or Dallas), where they then are transferred to a connecting flight. The advantage of this system is in its efficiency—it fills more seats. But hub-and-spoke scheduling increases the difficulty of an on-time departure.

If a plane headed to Atlanta is in Chicago, it has to wait for passengers and baggage to arrive from many other airports. If anything goes wrong with any feeder flight, the Atlanta departure is delayed or it loses its revenue advantage. So the on-time departure of these feeder flights complicates the Chicago crew's desire to have an on-time Atlanta departure.

American took that complexity one step further by altering the options from plane to plane on their fourteen different types of aircraft. For example, planes would have different seating patterns or different kinds of life rafts, to make a more efficient configuration for thirty types of flight destinations. In those days, American would make 2,500 flight segments in and out of their hub-and-spoke system (now it's closer to 3,900), using 900 aircraft, divided into 14 types of planes and 30 different setups. Any mechanical challenge anywhere in the chain of events would result in further delays, as another "appropriate" craft could be difficult to find.

What American needed to assure they would be able to maintain a higher percentage of on-time departures than any competitor was a system to make sure *every* employee (from mechanic to caterer) at *every* American station did *everything* they could to get their planes off on time.

Crandall's solution was to study all the required activities for an on-time departure—the pilot's piece, the cabin cleaner's piece, the ramp agent's piece, and so on—then set performance goals for each function. It was an awesome level of analysis, but the logic behind it was simple. If all the pieces of a process (like an on-time departure) are optimized, you should end up with a flawless result. The process is called total functional, or "pinpoint," accountability.

The basic logic of pinpoint accountability is that any business outcome can be made better if you identify each individual's responsibilities and make sure they know when they are performing below acceptable standards. As you read earlier, when individuals know the score they are compelled to do something about it.

To make sure every individual knew when they were below par, American created a performance analysis department with the computing power to track the minimum acceptable performance standards (MAPS) for on-time departures (as well as baggage handling and customer complaints). If a failure occurred, Crandall made his supervisors accountable for going back and deciding where in the twelve groups of employees the failure happened and fixing the process or the person. One field manager told Dr. Gittell, "Crandall wants to see the corpse."

Crandall didn't stop with the analysis and the scorecard. To help managers use this "pinpoint" accountability to generate more on-time departures, he called together a team of executives to draw up a $20-million leadership-empowerment training program.

"He wanted all the front-line managers to take more responsibility [for on-time departures, proper baggage handling, and fewer customer complaints] by making more decisions on the spot," said Lynne Heitman, the executive Crandall put in charge of this initiative. "It sounded great."

But just two weeks after completing the program, Heitman suspected that getting managers and front-line employees to take the initiative to have more on-time departures "was just never going to work." She saw holes in the application of total functional accountability, including managers who had a hard time identifying clear lines of control, coming to mutual agreement on targets, and giving useful feedback to subordinates. Under these less-than-ideal conditions, she predicted that total accountability and more on-time departures (through employee empowerment) would be "diametrically opposed."

A FLAWED SYSTEM

Heitman saw empowerment from a different perspective than did the other members of the leadership program. Twelve months earlier, she had left headquarters to experience the real world of "airplanes, passengers, and cargo" by taking a front-line job at American's Memphis station. That posting made her acutely sensitive to the many difficulties faced by real employees trying to get real airplanes off the ground on time.

"Senior management never fully appreciated how difficult it was to do a good job within the system they created," Heitman explained. For example, "They'd make the master schedule without any understanding of the physical facilities," Heitman remembered. "We'd get a schedule every six weeks and they [headquarters] would schedule fifteen planes on the ground, even though we only had twelve gates," Heitman said. "We'd have to call Dallas and say, 'Hey, guys . . . fifteen planes, twelve gates, fifteen—twelve. . . . It's not going to work.'"

To those at the front it looked as if headquarters didn't care if they did things the right way or not. According to Heitman, "They'd say, 'Oh, we'll fix that.' But they never did. They continued [to make the schedules] without the feedback processes they needed to ever get it right."

Heitman tried to talk to the executives about the obstacles they had created. But they always found an excuse, like someone who had learned to work around these impediments. They'd point and say, "Why do I have to change? Joe over there is doing great," Heitman said. According to Dr. Gerald Kraines, a lecturer at Harvard Medical School, this is a common conclusion for many managers. They see that some people "can, through sheer willpower, brute force and long hours—overcome managerial abdication, systemic dysfunctionality and structural flaws."* And they expect that everyone can do the same.

Heitman's reaction to this rationalization was "Well, Joe is a superstar, he's highly skilled, he's confident, and he knows how to work around any obstacles in the system. *Regular* people just give in." If you want people to take the initiative and make more decisions on their own, Heitman said, "you have to create an environment where *ordinary* managers and employees can get things done."

*Gerald A. Kraines, M.D., *Accountability Leadership*, Career Press, 2001.

Heitman asked a number of front-line employees why they didn't take more initiative and found another reason to suspect Crandall's empowerment program would fall far short of its goal.

"They shot right back," Heitman said. "'Are you kidding? The last guy who did that got fired.'"

According to Heitman, American's managers regularly resorted to fear tactics and intimidation, discouraging any feedback in the process.

"I worked for a guy in Nashville," Heitman said. "He was a vice president. He'd go to Dallas once a week and he'd get beat up. Then he'd come back and beat the crap out of us. We never knew why, we had no clue. [And] we were too scared to ask.

"[Another leader at American] was constantly saying how [he] encouraged debate and created an atmosphere where everyone felt safe offering their opinions even if they were contrary to his. But he was a bully . . . and he didn't have the ability to perceive his own [negative] impact."

Management's whole attitude about associates could be very harsh. "If people didn't take responsibility [for achieving performance goals], *they were weaklings*," Heitman said, characterizing the blaming mind-set of some top executives. "They were [just] bad people and incorrect hires for the company."

In response to this harsh attitude, she observed, "[Regular] people kept their heads down. Their number-one goal was to give their bosses just enough to keep them off their backs. On the front lines the prevailing attitude was 'How do I keep my ass out of the sling?' not 'How can I make a contribution to the big goal of an on-time departure?'"

Heitman saw that American was far from the ideal world of *The One Minute Manager*. Specifically:

1. Employees were asked to take accountability for situations they couldn't control.
2. Supervisors weren't skilled at providing "useful and constructive" feedback.

3. The big goal (an on-time departure) required employees to act
   as a team, (collaborating, coordinating, and cooperating), but
   pinpoint accountability, combined with the harsh attitudes of
   supervisors, had them all "looking out for number one."

The solution in Heitman's mind was as clear as the obstructions
she saw: Do a complete makeover to the top levels of management
in addition to the complete makeover they were doing to the front
lines. "If you want to decontaminate a pond, you can't just clean
each fish," she said, "you have to clean the whole ecosystem."
American needed to do more than tell the front lines how to take
more responsibility. "You can tell them what to do, but they are not
going to change until you change the way you measure them, com-
pensate them, and [especially] *the way you support them*," Heitman
said.

But true to the negative environment Heitman had uncovered,
headquarters didn't want to hear what they didn't like to hear. "My
boss thought I was a heretic for saying we are wasting twenty million dollars," Heitman said. HR's attitude was, if the top bosses
want workshops, we'll give them workshops.

But Heitman was still too enthused from the original vision
Crandall had communicated. "I believed I could change the world
[like Crandall did]," she said. So she asked for a transfer. "Give me
an operation and I'll show you."

BOSTON GETS A MAKEOVER

Lynne Heitman was transferred to the most difficult, most dysfunctional airport operation in American's portfolio. "Boston's Logan Airport was infamous," she explained. "Logan was the place GMs went
and just survived until they rotated out to a new location. The fact
that it ran at all was a miracle. Nobody thought it could be fixed.

"It [Logan] had a core group of hard-line, flamethrowing union
throwbacks who hated management and gave the entire Boston station a bad name."

But despite these negatives at Logan, Heitman was optimistic. "There were also a lot of people, union and otherwise, who wanted to do a good job," she observed.

Five hundred people were on her crew, all with a long history at the airline, including ground operations—ticket agents, gate personnel, and cargo (everyone with the job of getting flights off the ground on time except the mechanics)—plus flight attendants and pilots. They had all worked for years, for the most part doing their jobs with a minimum of enthusiasm.

Now Heitman was going to try what she learned and get them to show more individual initiative.

Her chance came quickly when American added their first international flight at Logan, a nonstop from Boston to London's Heathrow Airport. Instead of attempting to divide the work into individual tasks and use performance measures to see who was up to par, Heitman decided to emphasize communication, coordination, and cooperation, and practice every new idea American had developed for the empowerment training program.

"The key lesson in our leadership program was 'the people who do the work should design the process,'" Heitman explained. She organized a London team to figure out what would work best.

She gathered representatives from the bag room, maintenance, ticket counter, and ground crew to have a daily predeparture meeting. Everyone who had a vested interest in getting that flight off the ground had a voice.

Having different departments talk to each other was a new experience at Logan Airport. "A lot of companies morph into these little fiefdoms, and since they're not required to talk to each other . . . they don't," Heitman noted. That tendency was only made worse by American's combination of dysfunctional management attitudes and "pinpoint" accountability. "The lead agent upstairs and the crew chief downstairs had worked the same transcontinental [Boston to L.A.] flight every day for twenty years," but "they had never spoken to each other," Heitman said incredulously.

"But our London team met every day with an agenda. Just to talk through the simple things like 'Any problems with equipment?' Maintenance would say, 'Yeah, the aft door can't be used for loading passengers, so you have to load them from the front.' Just the little things like that made everything go smoothly," Heitman said.

Soon, Heitman started to see a big difference. "It [Boston to London] was by far the best-run departure we had going in and out of Logan," she recalled. "Hands down, the best service and the best on-time record.

"Everyone noticed that the front-line people who were handling that flight made the decisions and adjustments that needed to be made and coordinated the departure perfectly, getting the airplane off the ground with all the passengers and all the cargo on time," Heitman said proudly. "They got to know each other so well that if some unanticipated problem cropped up they'd call 'Bill' down in the bag room and they'd fix it themselves. They didn't need a manager there to tell them what to do. They thought of themselves as 'The London Flight Team,' which was a cool thing."

Heitman believed this was the result Crandall had in mind. True, she didn't get there through pinpoint accountability and using MAPS ratings to score each individual. But that wasn't because Crandall's functional accountability was a bad idea. It was simply out of sync with the existing environment. Managers at American didn't have good feedback skills and didn't understand the importance of teamwork (over functional accountability) to achieve the goal of more on-time departures.

Dr. Gittell explained why on-time departures were a bad choice for employing functional accountability: "[Pinpoint accountability] encourages optimization at the level of the individual function, which does not necessarily lead to achievement of the overall goal, particularly in highly interdependent work processes where performance of the overall process depends on what happens at the interfaces between the functions, as much as on what happens within the functions themselves."

In other words, when the goal is providing better customer service through more on-time departures, it's more important that everybody is talking and looking out for one another than that managers have a precise scorecard of who's accountable for any miscue.

But even following Heitman's documented success at their most difficult station, she couldn't persuade headquarters to consider a top-level makeover to get in sync with the demands of a more responsible/more empowered workplace. "It was going to take someone with more skill than I had to change the management style," she said.

Heitman left American Airlines. She turned her ability to recognize hidden motivations and her keen eye for people, conflicts, and human nature to writing novels. Today she's a successful author of three mystery-thrillers set in the airline business, *Tarmac, Hard Landing,* and *First Class Killing.*

And you already know the American Airlines side of the story. The airline that went on to make on-time departures and customer satisfaction their competitive advantage wasn't American—it was Southwest.

In 2001, Southwest generated one-sixth the level of complaints as American Airlines and other major carriers (measured per million customer miles). Southwest created more loyal customers, more loyal employees, and better profitability than the rest of the airline industry. The carrier was number one in punctuality for most of the nineties, and whereas the heightened security after 9/11 caused Southwest a temporary period of flight delays, they were bouncing back to the top of the pack in the fall of 2002.

Most important, they achieved their success, according to Dr. Gittell (who wrote *The Southwest Airlines Way,* published in 2003), specifically by backing away from pinpoint accountability, discouraging finger-pointing, and coaching managers on providing *useful* feedback, just as Heitman did during her Logan Airport experience.

The lesson is clear: Rather than blindly assuming that keeping score will always help you reach your goals, managers need to find the line between enough and too much accountability. By never crossing that line, they can avoid undermining their people's individual initiative.

HOW TO "FIND THE LINE"

As you can imagine, there can be no single, hard-and-fast rule for deciding how much accountability is enough and how much is too much. You have to develop a real feel for the expectations you are trying to meet or exceed, and assess the strengths and weaknesses of your working environment just as Lynne Heitman did.

Start by matching your organization to the definition of accountability in an ideal workplace: *Accountability is a partnership, where smart, creative, and hardworking managers divide big expectations into clearly understood pieces, then mutually agree with an individual or a group that the latter will take responsibility for their part. The manager then follows up with useful and constructive feedback.*

Now assess your ability to deliver on the critical adverbs and adjectives of accountability in that definition. Are your targets and paths *clearly* understandable and *clearly* achievable? Can you get *mutual* agreement? Do your managers follow up?

Are the degrees of accountability you plan to use *fair*? Ask yourself:

- **How much control will the group or individual have over the outcomes?** Holding someone accountable without knowing if they can control their outcomes is unfair. Remember the case at American where management scheduled fifteen planes into a facility with only twelve gates. Holding that local crew accountable for any delays when they didn't have enough gates to meet their goal would have been plainly unfair. Any perceived or real unfairness has a bad effect on initiative.

- **How good are the managers at giving useful feedback?** If a manager can't provide useful performance critiques either because they are stretched too thin or lack the attitudes or skills to be a good coach, they need to be especially careful about their demands for tight accountability.

- **What is more important to achieving your goals—pinpoint accountability or communication, cooperation, and coordination?** At times, it's more important that everybody talks to one another than that managers keep score of who's accountable for a misstep.

- **Lastly, don't accept the conventional wisdom that says accountability is a panacea.** All managers want absolutes. It's the natural reaction to all the stress of working in fast-changing, high-stakes situations. But each work scenario needs to be judged individually—there is no one right answer.

Now you have an uncomplicated three-step criterion for assessing each situation and finding the line between enough and too much accountability. Use it.

Conclusion

■

IT'S NOT WHAT YOU SAY . . . IT'S WHAT YOU DO THAT MAKES THE DIFFERENCE

Somewhere between 32 and 94 percent of your customers are thinking about switching to your competition.

If you're in the insurance industry, about a third of all your clients are ready to make the leap. More than half are at risk if you provide cell phone or banking services. In a department or specialty apparel store, four out of five customers are contemplating a change. And if you run a fast-food franchise, you're on the verge of losing 94 out of every 100 customers who bought a burger last week.

It's no better in professional and industrial sectors. Fifty-five percent of enterprise software-solutions buyers are antsy, and 61 percent of executives who outsource say they'd love to find someone else to buy from.

There are several factors that can push clients over the edge. Curiosity (when your buyer asks himself, "Am I getting the best deal?"), inducement (when a competitor asks your customers, "Would you like to see a much better deal?"), or even chance (when circumstances put your clients and your competition in the same place at the same time)—all are known to prompt customer defection.

But one factor is the gateway for all the others. It's disappointment—the feeling of outrage and regret a company creates when its regulars don't get what they expected. Disappointment is the catalyst for defection.

Think about it. You are bombarded with about 3,000 advertising inducements every day. They mostly go in one ear and out the other. But the day your credit-card company disappoints you, you will actually stop and pay attention to the ad offering a *zero percent finance charge* on balance transfers from another financial institution. The same goes for your phone service, your software supplier, or any other commercial relationship.

It's very expensive to replace an existing customer. Not only does a company have to pay through the nose to find fresh prospects, but the discounts or other giveaways necessary to get people to switch take a big bite out of any organization's current operating margins. Then, as any employee from the front lines will tell you, that new customer will ask more questions and demand more attention, straining already stretched customer-support budgets to the breaking point.

It's an undeniable fact of doing business—new customers cost more and pay back less than do existing clients. That's why the most effective cost-saving move a manager can make is to stop doing anything at any level that causes current customers to feel disappointed.

Which brings us back to how following through at every level can make or break your company. You can't stop people from being curious or keep your competitors from dangling a carrot. But you can stop all the dropped balls and unforced errors that disappoint your good customers (or key employees and best investors), any of which could become the *straw that breaks the back* of a long-term, profitable customer relationship.

Everything you need to create this new level of thoroughness and reliability under the toughest competitive conditions is now in your hands. That puts you 98 percent of the way home. The final 2 percent comes after you shore up your company's attitude about keeping their commitments.

HOW STRONG IS YOUR COMMITMENT?

It was early evening in a Hong Kong restaurant when a customer's cell phone rang. On the other end was a caller with shocking news: A plane had just flown into the World Trade Center.

It's probably an accident, Leslie Robertson thought as he overheard that conversation, like in 1945 when a B-25 bomber lost in the fog mistakenly collided with the Empire State Building. Robertson and his partner, John Skilling, had anticipated just such a mishap when they did the original structural engineering for the twin towers back in 1966.

Returning to his hotel room, however, the WTC designer discovered the awful truth. Two hijacked jetliners had been commandeered and flown like missiles into the North and South Towers. Both buildings were leveled and almost 3,000 people were dead.

Less than a month later, Robertson stood before the National Council of Structural Engineers to share his thoughts on the collapse of his innovative design.

"Here you can see classical tension failure," he said, pointing to slide after slide of twisted steel, jagged exterior panels, and piles of rubble at Ground Zero. Robertson spoke clinically, like a medical examiner narrating an autopsy. "Next slide," he continued. "You can see the columns displaced. Welds are sheared off. Classical failures."

Robertson finished his prepared text and the moderator opened the floor for questions. "Is there anything you wish you had done differently in the design of the building?" an attendee shouted unexpectedly. The room went silent as the matter-of-fact session turned into an emotional experience.

"I guess I wish I had made it stand up longer," the engineering wunderkind replied. His voice quaked and was reduced to a whisper: "I mean, every man was important." Then, as the *Wall Street Journal* reported, Robertson stopped, stood alone at the front of the room, and wept.

Robertson had done his best. He and his team designed the towers to withstand the chance impact of a Boeing 707, the largest aircraft imaginable in 1966. No one could reasonably expect him to have anticipated two hijacked Boeing 767s with more than 10,000 gallons of explosive jet fuel ramming nose-first into the ninety-fourth and seventy-eighth floors of his lower Manhattan monuments.

Yet Robertson couldn't escape feeling the anguish of not living up to everyone's expectations. "I have a lot of tough nights," he later told *The New Yorker*. "I go to sleep for a little bit, but I wake up thinking. . . . Had I done a bit more . . . Had the towers stood up for just one minute longer . . . I have so many thoughts."

On the WTC commemorative Web site next to Robertson's picture is a quote that explains why he obsesses: *The robustness and stamina of the buildings is my responsibility. All the drawings have my name on them.*

Every manager at your company needs to hear the story of Leslie Robertson. Robertson represents the kind of commitment that spurs 100 percent follow-through.

The average businessperson demonstrates an average amount of commitment. They stick to their promises as long as things are going as planned. But when things don't, they fall back on excuses. For example:

I called an office products company. Their ad promised same-day delivery for printer supplies. "Yes, your cartridge is in stock," the company told me, "but you've got to understand, our delivery schedule is full. Would you mind if we got it to you in a day or two?"

Another time, I dialed my "anywhere" cell phone from my house and ended up nowhere. "You've got to understand," customer service told me when I reached them using my home phone, "reception can be spotty even in our guaranteed coverage areas. Why don't you try calling again from another location."

In still another incident, I waited ninety minutes for a scheduled appointment that never happened. "You've got to understand," said the no-show executive when I asked what happened, "the deputy president called me into a meeting, my assistant dropped the ball on a major business report, and time just got away from me. Can we reschedule our get-together?"

"You've got to understand" makes it all too easy to accept the conditions that disappoint customers and lead to their defection. Take the recent history at Sun Microsystems, for example:

> At the end of 2002, the chief information officer at Reliant Resources bought some gear from Sun. After signing the contract, he found himself having to talk to three or four different installations people and going over the same issues over and over again. "They lost their customer focus," the disappointed CIO later told the *Wall Street Journal*.
>
> A Sun spokeswoman tried to explain why. Sun was revamping all their operations in response to the worldwide crash in tech purchasing. When a company like Sun makes big structural changes, she told the *Journal*, it is expected to have some "managed chaos." In other words, Sun's customers should "understand" if there's a gap between what Sun says and what they do.
>
> But many customers didn't understand. In 2003, Sun's product sales were down 40 percent from their peak even as other tech companies were recovering from the tech downturn.

Leslie Robertson didn't ask anyone to understand. Even though he had done his best and the cause of the collapse was an unimaginable, once-in-a-billion event, he was racked by personal feelings of responsibility. It's those feelings that act as the catalyst for a real, sustained, and committed effort to follow through. (Sun stopped asking its customers "to understand" shortly after those events in 2002 and has since instituted thirty new initiatives to show they are dead serious about delivering on their commitments.)

James Crowe, the CEO of Level 3 Communications, has learned the hard way that following through on commitments (especially when things don't go as planned) is an organization's biggest challenge. "You can say all you want, you can send e-mails and memos," he explained, "but if it [keeping commitments] is not built into the way your people think about themselves and each other, it won't happen."

Crowe is currently guiding one of the few companies that are still following through on the promised revolution in high-speed communications.

From 1996 to 2000, investors poured $757 billion into companies offering fiber-optic and other kinds of solutions for moving data at the speed of light—Level 3, Global Crossing, Qwest Communications, 360 Networks, Williams, Genuity, Winstar, WorldCom, and others. Then the tech bubble burst. "By our count," Crowe said, "about ninety competitors have declared bankruptcy."

In other words, when the going got tough the vast majority of companies forgot their many obligations to customers, employees, and investors and instead looked out for number one. You've read their stories. They have filled the pages of the business press and even a few federal court transcripts.

But Crowe and the people at Level 3 didn't seek bankruptcy protection from their commitments. They took an immense hit when the bubble burst. But instead of dodging their responsibilities, they took a deep breath and recommitted themselves to maintaining customer service and rebuilding the trust of customers, employees, and investors.

"You do what it is that you say you're going to do," Crowe said. Level 3's management is on the same track as the managers interviewed for this book—clear expectations, more accurate assessments, creating HOT teams, showing respect, and especially sharing their purpose, "to become the network partner you can rely on."

But what has led Crowe and his executive team to take this path less traveled? It was the same feelings of personal responsibility that Robertson felt. "We had an obligation," Crowe explained. "We owed our investors. We owed our customers. We owed our employees. Plus we believe in the market."

Commitment means never asking the other side "to understand." All managers must be willing to expose themselves (like Robertson and Crowe) and say, "The robustness and stamina of the follow-through is my responsibility. All our promises have my name on them."

Acknowledgments

When Buffy Caflisch of Watson Wyatt Worldwide saw her story told in the chapter "Lead a HOT Team," she was concerned. "I know, it's your storytelling style to give the credit [for simplicity's sake] to one person's vision. But I want to be clear that this isn't all due to me. The only reason we are as far ahead as we are is because of the active involvement of so many people in the practice in trying to continuously improve our approach. They deserve a good share of the credit."

And so it is for every leader who's shared their insights with you throughout this book. It is therefore only right to acknowledge *all* the people at IKEA, Yellow Roadway Transportation, Level 3 Communications, SSM Health Care, the *Wall Street Journal,* Pella Corporation, Union Square Hospitality Group, Watson Wyatt, TBM Consulting, IDEO, Charles Schwab, Fairmont Hotels and Resorts, Garcia Media, and BluePoint Energy, Inc., for their unsung contributions to cracking the code of follow-through.

Additionally, I should thank the scores of executives and middle managers who shared the tales of their company's trials and tribulations anonymously. They were concerned about headquarters' reaction, so they kept their names out. But without their insights (and their candor), I would have lacked a critical element of good judgment. As Will Rogers explained, "Good judgment is the result of experience, and a lot of that comes from bad judgment."

Lastly, there are many others who deserve credit for helping me behind the scenes. Some initiated an idea, others coordinated my efforts, and still others acted as a sounding board or (unknowingly) gave me a blisteringly honest critique that inspired me to make my points that much clearer.

They also should be acknowledged.

Thanks to Jason Jennings, Tenney Campbell, Clive Cashman, Suzanne Dawson, John Constantine, Hannah Kluger, Diane Baier, Michael Hershey, Ed Jenks, Jay Farr, Jim Yager, Marc Gibeley, Susan Clark, Vince Thompson, Stephanie Land, Michael Traynor, John Ryan, Jade Harrison, Ben Bahn, David McDonald, Tricia Petruney, Kendra Harpster, Robert Medearis, Dixie Platt, Ken Harris, Joe Blythe, Tom Manz, Jack Covert, Chris Cornelius, John Williams, Stacey Lawson, R. Bradshaw, Jenny Zinman, Dave Trabert, Harry Hertz, Ronnie Bauch, Ray Schonbak, Alexandra Holder, Anne Cole, and Roger Scholl.

Thanks to my family, Robbie, Nick, and Nancy, who made it possible for me to write, and to my parents, Loretta and Ray, who made it impossible for me to strive for anything less than 100 percent follow-through.

Index